D0018681

Finding Home

Finding Home

Stories of Roman Catholics Entering the Episcopal Church

Christopher L. Webber

COWLEY PUBLICATIONS
Cambridge ✦ Boston
Massachusetts

Library of Congress Cataloging-in-Publication Data:
Webber, Christopher L.
    Finding home: stories of Roman Catholics entering the Episcopal church / Christopher Webber.
        p.   cm.
    Includes bibliographical references.
    ISBN 1-56101-133-9 (alk. paper)
    1. Anglican converts—United States—Biography. 2. Episcopal Church—Biography.   3. Anglican Communion—United States—Biography.   4. Episcopal Church—Membership. 5. Anglican Communion—United States—Membership. 6. Catholic Church—United States—Membership I. Title.
BX5990.W43   1996
283'.73—dc20   96-41781
                                                                                                            CIP

Cynthia Shattuck, editor.
Vicki Black, copyeditor and designer.

This book is printed on recycled, acid-free paper and was produced in Canada.

Cowley Publications
28 Temple Place
Boston, Massachusetts 02111
800-225-1534
http://www.cowley.org/~cowley

For my father,
from whom I first learned the Catholic faith

Contents

Preface

Every book is the product of a community. If it is fiction, it comes from the author's experience of human life in community. If it is nonfiction, it relies on information drawn from many sources, whether recognized or unrecognized. This book draws first of all on my experience of community life in the Episcopal Church, but it is the result more specifically of help from particular individuals. Those whose stories are told in this book have been patient in answering my questions and helpful in reading what I had written and correcting my misunderstandings. The one exception was Matthew Fox, who was at work on his own story already and understandably preferred to tell it himself in his own way. Nevertheless his assistant, Peter Faraday, was most helpful in providing material and answering questions.

I am grateful to Fred Barbee, Kim Byham, John Rodgers, Roger White, and Susan Mills for help in finding people whose stories would present as complete a range of experience as possible. Brendan McCormack, Roger White, Stephen Parker, Robert Ladehoff, Jan Mulryan, Dennis Gagnon, and Susan Mills were gracious in helping round out the stories in which they had played a role. Helen Johnson, Bishop Lamb's administrative assistant, provided helpful materials and Caroline Webber did research for me. Elena Barnum gave generously of her time in reading my manuscript and suggesting numerous improvements. Cynthia Shattuck gave encouragement and helped clarify the purpose of the book and shape it more clearly toward that purpose. And once again,

Margaret, my wife, has been my best proofreader, critic, and enabler. This is a better book because of the help this support community has given me. If I had paid closer attention to them, it might have been better yet!

The Church Catholic

The Catholic faith is that which has been believed always, everywhere, and by all. *(St. Vincent of Lerins)*

When someone says to me, "I was brought up Catholic," I often reply, "So was I." I am not a *Roman* Catholic and I never have been; I was brought up as an Episcopalian, but I never doubted that I belonged to the Catholic Church. And I did what Roman Catholics did: I went to mass, I ate fish on Fridays, I gave things up in Lent, I called the clergy "Father."

Of course, in the little country town in the western part of New York State where I grew up, there was no one to argue with me. Hardly anyone knew a Roman Catholic. There were, in fact, a few Roman Catholics in town: Mr. Quinn ran the newsstand and Tony Midey fixed our shoes when they were worn; on Ash Wednesday one or two children in my class would come to school with smudges on their foreheads. The little Roman Catholic church was only a few blocks away with its neatly trimmed lawn and its statue of the Virgin, but I never saw anyone go in or out and I have no memory of ever seeing the priest.

Not until I went away to college did I really meet a Roman Catholic. A friend of mine roomed with a man named McGee and I got to know him fairly well, but I still learned very little about his church. I did meet some priests, though, because I was a member of the college debate team. We had a busy schedule, traveling north as far as Boston and south as far as Georgia. We met the same teams with the same coaches at tournaments in Vermont and Boston and Pittsburgh and Washington. Fr. Murphy coached the team from St. Peter's College and Fr. O'Connell coached the team from Canisius College. Sometimes when the debates were over, we would go out together for something to eat and talk about many things. I remember thinking that Frs. Murphy and O'Connell made excellent representatives of their church: if they were Roman Catholics, there must be something very worthwhile about that church.

But I never considered joining the Roman Catholic Church. I suppose I might have spent my college years questioning my faith; it's an ordinary part of growing up and finding out what matters. But I was lucky enough to room with some men who thought they were atheists and who challenged my faith in a way that made me seek out arguments for my side and appreciate what I'd inherited. Pushed hard by atheists, the pull of Rome didn't have much chance. In fact, by the time my senior year rolled around, I had decided I wanted to go on to seminary and prepare myself for the priesthood.

Seminarians, of course, learn about church history and they learn about the Reformation. They learn about the divisions in the church. If they are Episcopalians, they learn about the claims of Rome and the reasons why Episcopalians reject those claims. I acquired a good deal of "book learning" in seminary—but never met a Roman Catholic to talk to about that learning.

So it was a rude awakening when I moved into my first parish in the Greenpoint section of Brooklyn. Greenpoint in those days was a blue-collar community of first-generation Americans, most of whom came from Ireland and Poland. Parish names were Logan, Cullom, McGinity, Riordan, and O'Keefe on the one hand, and Kilanowski, Leonowich, and Pawlukiewicz on the other. And remember, this was the *Episcopal* Church! Those with Irish names tended to be from the north of Ireland, Anglican by birth and tradition and loyal to William of Orange; those with Polish names, on the other hand, usually joined the church when they married an Episcopalian.

It was an interesting neighborhood. There were large Roman Catholic churches dedicated to eastern saints like Cyril and Methodius and Stanislas Kostka. There was also a Uniate congregation, part of a church whose background was shaped by turmoil in central Europe centuries ago. The Uniates were of Russian Orthodox background and had become affiliated with the Roman Catholic Church while retaining many of their own customs. They still used Old Church Slavonic in their liturgy; more important, their priests were allowed to marry. In addition, there was in our neighborhood a Russian Orthodox Church and a Polish National Catholic congregation. The latter is a church which became separated from the Roman Catholic Church in the late nineteenth century while still retaining almost all the traditions of Roman Catholicism, except the pope.

I remember calling on families and being told, "I'm an Episcopalian, Father, but my wife [or husband] is a Catholic." "Oh?" I would say. "What kind of Catholic?" This question usually drew a blank look—which was no surprise to me—and I would have an opportunity to do some teaching. "You see," I would say, "there are five kinds of Catholicism in this neighborhood: Russian, Polish, Roman, Uniate, and Anglican. We all have the sacraments and bishops who go back to the apostles. But we use different languages in the Mass and only the Roman Catholics and Uniates have a pope."

As a matter of fact, there were more kinds of Catholicism in Greenpoint than Protestantism. Two small Lutheran congregations, an even smaller Methodist church, and a storefront Baptist congregation were the lone representatives of the Reformation in our district. It wasn't very much like the little country town where I grew up, nor had I learned in upstate New York about the depth or intensity of the religious rivalries of Europe. Upstate we all pretty much got along, but Greenpoint was different. Let me tell you some stories.

There was (perhaps there still is) a tradition in Brooklyn of celebrating annually the organization of the first Sunday school in a Brooklyn church. Every year the Sunday schools of most of the non-Roman Catholic churches in Brooklyn held a parade. In Greenpoint it was a rather small parade, but the churches did the best they could. They carried banners and hired a Salvation Army band to lead them in what was called the "June Walk." I walked with the church school of the Church of the Ascension down Lorimer Street on a number of hot, early summer days.

Now Lorimer Street had one advantage as a parade site: it paralleled the main shopping street so it was conveniently located—but a parade didn't interfere unduly with traffic. Lorimer Street also had a big disadvantage: it ran directly behind St. Anthony's Church, the largest Roman Catholic Church in Greenpoint, and directly in front of St. Anthony's parochial school. Timing, as they say, is everything. A couple of years before I moved to Greenpoint, the June Walk was so timed that the children were parading past the parochial school just as school was ending for the day. Children poured out of the school to see other children going by in a parade carrying banners and marching to the blare of a brass band. The nuns were horrified. Responding alertly to the danger of the situation, they lined the parochial school children up on the sidewalk and made them turn their backs until the parade had passed.

It was while I was serving in Greenpoint that John XXIII became pope and summoned the Second Vatican Council. There was much excitement. I heard from children in our church that their Roman Catholic friends were saying, "The pope has called a council and now everyone is going to be Roman Catholic!" It wasn't that simple, of course, but it did make a difference. Perhaps ten years later someone sent me a clipping with a picture from the local paper of the institution of a new rector of the Church of the Ascension, Greenpoint, with a delegation of nuns from St. Anthony's Church in the procession. No longer turning their backs on our parade, they had come so far as to join it.

I learned some very practical things in Greenpoint. I learned, for example, that the differences among churches are often as much a matter of sociology as theology. I learned that religious affiliation is deeply interwoven with cultural patterns, that one's church membership is often part of a larger package. I learned that the religious part of the package is often the most emotional.

One woman of Irish ancestry in our congregation married a man of Irish ancestry who was a member of the Roman Catholic Church but quite willing to go to church with his wife and raise their children in the Episcopal Church. His family, however, was unable to accept the situation. They made life so hard for the new couple that the young woman had what used to be called a "nervous breakdown" and had to be hospitalized. When she came home she joined her husband's church. Such was the state of ecumenical relationships in Greenpoint forty years ago.

I learned one other thing in Greenpoint about the differences between our churches, and I learned it while standing on the front steps of the row houses that lined the streets there, waiting for someone to respond to my pushing of the doorbell. Houses in Greenpoint typically lean against each other and are four stories high. There were, of course, no elevators; neither was there an intercom system or a buzzer. Episcopalians, it seemed to me, always lived on the top floor. You pushed a doorbell and waited for someone to call down the stairs or out the window: "Who's there? Oh, Father! C'mon up." More than once, as I was standing on the steps awaiting the summons and watching a game of stickball on the street, I would hear one boy say to another, "Must be somebody dying; there goes the priest." So I learned that the Roman Church had far fewer priests per member than we did. I realized that that radically different ratio must radically affect church life—pastoral care and sense of community could hardly be the same if a priest only came to call when someone was dying.

I moved from Greenpoint to the suburbs, to a community on Long Island in which the Roman Church was still strong but somehow not as visible or dominating a presence. There was no inter-clergy organization, and I don't remember ever meeting the Roman Catholic clergy. I was invited to a mass at St. Raymond's when Pope John XXIII died, and I was given tickets to Yankee Stadium when Pope Paul VI came to New York. I remember the singing of the *Dies Irae* at the requiem and the reading of a lesson or prayer in Chinese at Yankee Stadium, but neither of these events provided insights into the nature of the Roman Catholic Church or the relationship between the two churches.

Six years in Japan as the rector of the English-language Anglican Church in Tokyo, however, brought me into contact with a remarkable man whose attitude toward the ecumenical movement significantly affected my own. Joseph Spae was a Belgian Roman Catholic priest who had founded the Oriens Institute to study the relationship between Japanese society and the Christian church. He gathered at the Institute a cross-section of clergy for a monthly ecumenical meeting. There were priests and ministers of every stripe: Roman and Anglican, Baptist and Lutheran, Mennonite and Southern Baptist. They were, for the most part, church officials or teachers of theology in local colleges and seminaries, and the discussions that took place were open-minded and thoughtful.

Fr. Spae was very realistic about denominational differences. "Tell me what church a Japanese goes to," he would say, "and I'll tell you who the first missionary was whom they met—or whom their parents met." He would rail against the way the churches had imposed on Japan the denominational differences formed in the West centuries earlier. "Why should the Christian church impose these differences on the Japanese?" he would question. No one could give him an answer.

I wish we could eliminate the obstacles to Christian unity and bury them with our history. I wish there were only one Catholic Church, indeed that there were only one church. But we remain divided. The divisions were created long ago over issues in many cases long dead, and they have shaped very different ways of Christian living. We share a common faith; we share a similar pattern of worship and ministry. But we differ in important ways so that, while some people remain at home in the church of their upbringing, others find themselves seeking another, and for a variety of reasons.

What is it like, then, to come into a new church for the first time? Why do people come and what do they find? I will try to answer these questions by telling stories of people who have been there. This is a book about people who began as Roman Catholics and eventually found their way to the Episcopal Church. They are all kinds of people: priests and lawyers, business people and homemakers. Some have become priests in the Episcopal Church, others are active in their new home as members of committees and parish officers, still others just go to church and say their prayers and try to live Christian lives. Their stories, I believe, tell as much or more about the Episcopal Church and the Roman Catholic Church as many volumes of theology, highlighting the ways in which the Episcopal Church and the Roman Catholic Church are similar, and the ways they are different. By listening to their stories we all may be able to come to a clearer understanding of what it means to be Roman Catholic, Anglo-Catholic, and plain Catholic—and even what it means to be a Christian.

A striking feature of the stories these former Roman Catholics tell about their experience of the Episcopal Church is their sense that they have "come home." Surely they do not mean that they have found again the things that might distinguish Roman Catholicism from other kinds of Catholicism or Christianity: the statuary, the lace-fringed cottas, the emphasis on the Virgin Mary and the cult of saints, the authority of the pope. No, what they are talking about is their discovery of a church which has very little that is distinctively its own, in which the fundamentals are few but solidly in place. Those fundamentals are the same they had known in the Church of Rome, and the fundamentals are what identify the Episcopal Church as home.

Their reasons for leaving the Roman Catholic Church are as different as the paths that led them to the Episcopal Church. But there are some common threads that weave through the stories. In following those threads, I hope that newcomers to the Episcopal Church will find it easier to understand their new home and become more comfortable with it. I hope that Roman Catholics and Episcopalians who are in dialog will come to understand themselves and each other better. And I hope that Episcopalians, seeing their church through the eyes of others, may be better able to welcome newcomers and help them feel at home.

Finally, it is my hope that these stories will also help point to issues for dialogue between the churches, moving us toward the future Matthew Fox has glimpsed: a post-denominational, re-united church which is neither Roman nor Anglican but Catholic, Orthodox, and Reformed: simply the Catholic Church, the universal home to which God is calling us all.

1

Coming In

Hope Adams and Jerry Lamb

"I had come to the place where I belonged." *(Hope Adams)*

The Catholic faith is this: that we worship....
(The Athanasian Creed)

Hope Adams remembers very clearly the first time she walked down the aisle to receive communion at a non-Roman Catholic altar. "As I walked forward, I saw in my mind's eye ahead of me the rectangle in the floor that might truly open up and swallow me!"

Belonging to a church is serious business. Church membership is part of our identity, a matter of who we are, like being a member of a particular family or being an American. None of these loyalties is easily given up. Family membership may change as we grow up, leave home, and form a family of our own, but we still belong to the family of our birth. Being an American or Canadian or German may have to do only with earthly loyalties, but few, indeed, renounce their citizenship carelessly. Nor do we easily give up being a Roman Catholic or an Episcopalian or a Baptist or a Lutheran. Church membership has to do with our relationship with God and our eternal destiny. Changing from one church to another can be frightening.

The documents of Vatican II affirm that in the "separated churches" the Holy Spirit is at work and salvation can be found, so why should people be afraid? Hope Adams believes that her own fear had several sources: "I don't know that I was ever taught specifically that going into another house of worship was wrong, but it was implicit in the instruction we were given," she remembers. Hope was taught that there was only "one true church," and therefore even to attend another church was to give credence to a different tradition, to imply that a "rival belief" was in some way valid. "The implicit message of the nuns," she recalls, "was that we were a church under siege and we shouldn't traffic with the enemy. It's a wonderful way to build a church; churches always do well under persecution."

Second, Hope feared that a new church might make demands she couldn't meet. In the Roman tradition she knew, "the answers were all there. I could accept them or reject them, but I was neither encouraged nor allowed to come up with my own ideas. The Prayer Book baptismal service asks God to give the candidate 'an inquiring and discerning heart'; there was nothing like that in any of the prayers I knew before."

Her third fear in finding a new church had to do with the loss of the faith of her past. "There was the fear," she acknowledges, "that something important to me, some of my experiences and personal pieties, would be rejected or discounted, and I didn't want to discard them. I wasn't rejecting my past; I was looking for a place to grow."

Hope Adams walked slowly over that invisible rectangle in the floor—and nothing happened. Safely across, she knelt and received communion. She had received communion many times before, but this time was different. "For the first time it wasn't just a magic cookie, but truly the body and blood of Christ. I felt a childlike glee that I didn't have to keep searching; I had come to the place where I belonged."

But if it had been hard for Hope to walk up the aisle of an Episcopal Church, it was even harder to tell her parents what she had done. Her mother was embarrassed: "Oh, what will I tell Aunt Mabel?" she worried. Her father, on the other hand, was simply baffled: "What? You left and you didn't *stay away?*" He had yearned, she believed, to take that step himself: not to break away from God—he was very close to God—but from the church whose teaching and practice he had always questioned.

There were others to be told as well when she joined her new church's inquirers' class and decided to be received into the Episcopal Church. She felt she must tell the priests who had been involved in her life: the priest who performed her marriage, the priest who had baptized her children, and others whose ministry had been significant to her. Her friends said, "Don't be silly, Hope. You're a big girl and you can make your own decisions." But there was a feeling of obligation. She called several priests she had known and told them what she planned to do and they, too, said, "It's your decision."

But she couldn't find the priest who had solemnized her marriage. He was no longer at the church where she and her husband Dan were married and no one seemed to know where he was. "He's not at this station anymore," they told her. "Don't worry about it," her friends urged her. "You don't need to tell him anyway." But Hope was persistent and finally she found him. He had left the priesthood and married. "Don't do it," he said. "You can't leave the church." For him, as for many others, there was no alternative to the Roman Catholic Church; it remained the only "real" church. If you were dissatisfied or unable to accept the rules, you might stay home on Sunday but there was nowhere else to go.

But Hope truly believed that she had found an alternative—indeed, for her, something better. When the bishop came in the spring, she walked up the aisle again and this time she was invited to kneel and receive a blessing. She had made the change. She was no longer a Roman Catholic. But the bishop who laid hands on her head in blessing stated very clearly that she was still a Catholic: "Hope," he said, "we recognize you as a member of the one holy catholic and apostolic Church, and we receive you into the fellowship of this Communion."

Becoming an Episcopalian means becoming a member of a world-wide church or "communion" which calls itself Catholic but not Roman. It is, you might say, more like a change within the family than a change to a new family. The English Catholic Church, unlike the Catholic churches of Italy and France, separated from the papacy in the sixteenth century and developed its own traditions. It has become, in the centuries since then, a world-wide family of churches of which the Episcopal Church is the American member. What Hope Adams and many others have found in the Episcopal Church is a place where they can be Catholics still, but with some important differences.

How do Roman Catholics come to the Episcopal Church for the first time? How did Hope Adams find her way there? Although you might begin Hope's story as she walked down the aisle of an Episcopal Church for the first time, the story really begins long before that—with childhood experiences and parental attitudes. The Holy Spirit usually works slowly and patiently through all our experience, and so quietly that we seldom notice until something happens that really gets our attention and forces a decision. Hope's story may be typical.

For Hope Adams the journey led from a Roman Catholic convent school to membership and then priesthood in the Episcopal Church. It has been a long journey and not an easy one. Why should God plant an instinct deep in the soul of a normal Roman Catholic child which can only be fulfilled at such cost?

"When I was four years old," Hope remembers, "I used to save Necco wafers and give communion to the dog and cat. Of course, I knew I couldn't really be a priest so the instinct got redirected. I thought I wanted to be a nun, but it never felt right. I knew I couldn't take a vow of obedience to anyone but God. I always had a deep sense of God's presence, something I didn't have words for and couldn't ask about."

The conflicting pulls were there, apparently, from the very beginning. On the one hand, a strong Roman Catholic background: three Roman Catholic grandparents, parents who went to mass every Sunday, the best education the church could give. But on the other hand, a nagging feeling that there was more, that questions were not being answered.

Of course, an alert and observant child will respond to the tiniest hint, and conflicting hints came at Hope from all directions. Yes, her parents seemed typically devout parishioners and made sure their daughter got a proper upbringing in the faith, but there was something else to notice as well. It was very much part of that faith as they practiced it that they went to mass every Sunday—and always left mass early to have a cigarette and get the Sunday paper. Such behavior sends a message. Or, perhaps, it sends two messages.

It may, in fact, be part of the tradition of American Roman Catholicism to go regularly to mass and yet complain and question afterwards. Hope's father did that. "He gave me permission to question," says Hope, "by his own questioning." When he didn't agree with something he would say bluntly, "That's a lot of baloney." Harold Howlett, Hope's father, questioned the church at home, yet in his privacy he had a deeper relationship with God than his formal relationship in the church. All his life, he prayed every night. Even toward the end of his life, when he began to drift away from the regular pattern of mass every Sunday, he said his prayers. If anything, his devotional life became deeper as his formal participation became less frequent. God was a part of his life, and perhaps it was the very security of that deeply personal relationship that allowed him to question, and allowed his daughter to question too.

A convent school is designed to form children's faith through instruction and guidance. Questioning is not a standard part of the curriculum. But Hope had questions. She remembers asking a nun what the circumcision was. The nun had an answer: "It was the first time Jesus shed his blood for us." If Hope had questions, the nuns did have answers, but they weren't always satisfying answers. There was no encouragement to ask questions or look for answers independently. Especially Hope was taught that ordinary people should not read the Bible because they would only get hopelessly confused.

Given the experience of Irish Roman Catholics both in Ireland and America, it may not be surprising that the faith taught in convent school was a faith to protect you from a hostile world, not a faith to open you to the love of God. "The Bible," she says, "seemed to be used as ammunition against the enemy." And prayer, too, was a means of defense against danger. Hope can still recite some of the prayers she learned to guide and protect her, as in this prayer to be said before going out on a date:

Tonight, O Lord, I wish to be,
The girl whom you would wish me to be
If I were to spend with thee
The morrow in eternity.

She also learned "custody of the eyes," though she can't remember exactly what it was that she was not supposed to look at. "It was just a feeling that you never know what you're going to see and it might be dangerous, so keep your eyes downcast and don't look around—especially in church." Was there something, she wondered, that you might see in church that was even more dangerous than what you might see outside?

Hope's parents moved often, from one suburb to another: suburban Wilmington, Chicago, New York. Seeking a good life for themselves, they sought a good life for their only child also: not a mere parochial school, but always the best, a convent school. And it gave her a certain feeling of security and continuity in the midst of change: always the same nuns, the same curriculum, the same mass. Children need to find stability and the convent schools provided it. Hope responded to that reassuring stability with the growing conviction that she was called to be a nun.

But that was not what her parents had in mind. By the time Hope was finishing eighth grade, she was able to express her sense of vocation. She was very serious about it and her parents responded seriously: they moved her into public school immediately. Hope had an aunt who took religion seriously, too, with holy cards and novenas. The family ridiculed her: "Religion has its place, but let's not get carried away!" Aunt Mabel's attempts to answer some of Hope's questions about religion were not appreciated by other members of the family. "Lay off," they told her. "Don't make the child too pious." Maybe the public school, where there were lots of boys and no nuns, would turn Hope's mind in a healthier direction.

Public school children, of course, still had "CCD" (the Confraternity of Christian Doctrine), the classes provided for them at the church after regular school hours. Hope was in high school now and still asking questions. A movie star had died after a life of prototypical Hollywood dissipation: wine, women, and song. The priest in charge of CCD thought it would be an excellent negative moral example to hold before the students. "It was God's judgment," said the priest. But Hope knew of other movie stars who had not met such a judgment. They had enjoyed wine, women, and song and lived to a ripe old age. How come? "How do you know it was God's judgment?" she asked. It was one question too many. The priest called her father and said that enough was enough: "She's not coming back." Nor did she. Some parents might have been angry to find their child expelled from religious classes, but Mr. Howlett was quietly pleased. The daughter who was unacceptable for CCD would obviously never be a nun. What a relief!

As for Hope, too pious for her family and too skeptical for the priest, faith now became a private matter. And it did still matter. She would sneak out of the house on weekday mornings to go to mass. She hadn't questioned the faith, only the package in which it was being presented. But she knew no other package.

The time for college came, and with it new opportunities, new freedom, and new challenges. Hope went to the University of Rochester, a quiet, liberal arts college in upstate New York. For some, college provides a chance to question and break with whatever religion has been passed on by the family. For Hope it was an opportunity to grow. The Newman Club provided Roman Catholic students with a place where questions could be asked—and answered. There was a good chaplain to help students think about their faith intelligently. No one told her to be quiet and stop asking questions. There were retreats to go on, speakers to listen to, discussion groups to take part in.

Academic work was exciting as well. Along with wanting to be a nun, Hope had also wanted to be a nurse. Just as being a nun was a substitute for her real vocation to priesthood, so being a nurse was an attainable version of a deeper desire to be a doctor. Hope had read not only the lives of the saints but also the lives of nurses; there were no women doctors to read about. By the time Hope went off to college, however, the passion to be a doctor was no longer out of reach for a woman and Hope could set her course for medical school. Her parents were well aware of her ambition. While her mother said, "Girls don't do that," her father was supportive: it was surely better than being a nun!

Hope remembers that first year of college as a wonderful time. Biology classes, in particular, brought the excitement that comes with a real discovery of vocation, a challenge that brings out one's best. "I felt like worlds had opened up to me," Hope recalls. She wrote home trying to convey her excitement and joy for her growing spirituality. "I feel as if I'm riding the crest of a wave," she told her parents.

Her father was not thrilled: obviously the University of Rochester was too liberal a place and something would have to be done about it. Hope, it seemed to him, was being influenced in a very unhealthy direction and he needed to block that influence before it was too late. She came home from her first year in college to find that her parents had arranged for a transfer. For her sophomore year she would go to Northwestern University in Chicago. Her father's roots were in the midwest; Chicago would be a safer environment. "I sent you to college to learn to buy bread," Mr. Howlett told his daughter, "and you can't buy bread with ideas."

So Hope went to Chicago feeling, she says, "lost and betrayed and not understood." But the next three years were "absolutely invaluable." Northwestern, too, was a place of freedom and opportunity, and Hope began to make discoveries that her father had never dreamed of. For one thing, Hope discovered the Episcopal Church.

Not far from Northwestern is Seabury-Western Seminary, a theological school where men (in those days) were prepared for the priesthood of the Episcopal Church. Since Episcopal clergy can marry, Episcopal seminarians sometimes went to the same parties as young women from Northwestern. Thus Hope met a seminarian. "He was kind of stuffy," she remembers, "but he intrigued me. He was connected with this other church that was a lot like *the* church. There was a sense of doing something a little risky and adventuresome."

One day, in this pursuit of adventure, Hope walked into St. Luke's Church, an Episcopal church not far from the campus of Northwestern, "and it was the beauty of holiness." She sat down and felt it: the austere, gothic arches, the vested altar with its candles, the stained glass. It was everything she had known from her life in the Roman Catholic Church and yet she felt a difference. She went back on Sunday after attending the Newman Club mass; after all, whatever St. Luke's might be, it wasn't the "real" church. But it was surprisingly similar and it held a certain fascination. She went again and sat in the back with a missal in one hand and the *Book of Common Prayer* in the other to make sure they were doing it right. As far as she could tell, they were.

Through the rest of her time at Northwestern Hope often went to two churches on Sunday. She always went to the Newman Club mass because "I knew I'd go to hell if I didn't go to mass." The fear of change had been deeply ingrained by now. But she went to St. Luke's and Atonement and other Episcopal churches too. She went to the services of Holy Week. "It felt like Thanksgiving dinner: so rich and wonderful. I wanted to sample everything." But she didn't write home about her discoveries. "I thought I'd wait," she explained. "I didn't want to upset them." If Hope's discoveries and excitement in Rochester had led to exile in Chicago, who knows what these new discoveries might have meant! It was not a risk to be taken lightly, and Hope kept her experiences in the Episcopal churches to herself. Hope graduated from Northwestern and returned to New York.

Medical school was still the goal, but would they accept her? Hope wasn't confident and decided at this point to take a year off. Her father knew someone who was setting up a program at the Sloane-Kettering Institute to do drug screening for anti-leukemic agents. That sounded perfect: a chance to pursue her career interest while postponing a final commitment. She would live in New York, explore the city, and learn about the real world.

Of course, if Rochester and Chicago are dangerous, New York is hardly a sanctuary. That first summer after college, Hope Howlett met Dan Adams, and Dan was an Episcopalian. Hope and four other girls ("We *were* girls," she emphasizes, "not women at all") had decided to find an apartment to share and needed a place to meet to plan their strategy. Someone knew a man called Dan Adams who had an apartment and would be happy to let them meet there to clip apartment ads and lay their plans. Dan was tall, dark, and handsome, and Hope fell in love. They were engaged in January, and married in June.

As an Episcopalian, Dan went to St. James' Church, Madison Avenue. Hope loved it. It seemed as if she were being led, one logical step at a time, into the Episcopal Church. But God is not always logical. Long and painful detours (God's straight road often seems like a detour to us) still lay ahead. To begin with, Dan had a complicated background. His grandmother, Vera Osborne Jenkyn, was English and stiffly proud of it. Roman Catholics, she thought, were generally Irish and of the servant class. One didn't get involved with the servants. Oddly, she herself had married an Italian Roman Catholic, much older than she, and she had learned to hate the Church of Rome and all its ways. She and her husband had agreed to parcel out their children by sex: boys would go with him, girls with her. The first two children were boys and they began their education with Jesuit tutors. Vera Osborne Jenkyn Gerli hated it. Two girls came along and were sent to the Brearley School in Manhattan for a proper upper-class New York education.

Dan's grandmother never got over her hatred of the Church of Rome and she was horrified to learn that Dan was planning to marry a Roman Catholic. She let it be known that she would disinherit him if he did what she had done. Mrs. Gerli had a significant amount of money, so disinheritance was no light threat. But would Dan give up the woman he loved for the sake of inheritance? Of course not. "I love Hope," he said, "and I will certainly not give her up for any amount of money." The wedding took place. Mrs. Gerli, very angry, came and sat in the back and left after the service. She did not attend the reception and she did not change her mind. Poor, proud, and happy, Dan and Hope went off to make a family and a future without Mrs. Gerli's money. As for Hope, whatever idea she might have had of joining Dan in the Episcopal Church was swept away in the turmoil. "How could I become an Episcopalian," she asked, "if Dan had given up his inheritance to marry a Roman Catholic?"

And how could plans for medical school fit into married life and a family? "I didn't give up medical school easily," Hope recalls, "not until after at least two children." But there wasn't much time even to think about it as three boys were born and the family moved to Bronxville, one of New York City's more prestigious suburbs. Dan worked in advertising, doing well but not satisfied. He drove himself hard. He wanted his own company. And he was drinking too much. But he was willing to work with Hope at the task of bringing children up in the faith. They went to St. Joseph's Church, Bronxville, as a family—Dan knew that Hope's strong Roman Catholic background made it certain he would go with her, not she with him—and before long Hope was teaching CCD and Dan was playing guitar for the family folk mass. He took instruction secretly, as a surprise for Hope. At the midnight Christmas mass, when the time came for communion, Dan walked up the aisle with Hope. "Merry Christmas; my present for you!" At last they could be one family with one church.

Two events brought matters to a climax. First, Hope had been teaching her CCD class about some of the divisions in the church and she had taken them to other churches to see for themselves what they were like. Two long blocks from St. Joseph's was Christ Church (where I was the rector at the time). She took her class there one day and when she walked in the memories of the church she had first encountered in Evanston were here also and its appeal was stronger now than before. In an odd way, it felt like home.

In the second place, one of the boys was now in first communion class and the parents were brought together for instruction in the new approach to the sacrament of confession. Now, they were told, it should be understood as a tool for growth rather than just a mechanical way to get rid of sins. Now there would be opportunity for dialogue in comfortable reconciliation rooms instead of the old dark confessional booths.

It sounded good to Hope and she decided to go to confession for the first time in years. The reconciliation rooms had not yet been created so the booths were still in use, but that was all right with her. The setting didn't matter as much as the opportunity to talk with a wise and understanding counselor about the apathy that seemed to be controlling her spiritual life. So she went into the booth and confessed to the sin of apathy. Apathy? Isn't that a lot like sloth, one of the seven deadly sins? Might there not be something here for a priest to get his teeth into and an opportunity to guide a penitent into real spiritual growth?

"Apathy?" said the priest behind the grille. "That doesn't sound like a matter for confession to me. Now, there are others waiting, so let's not tie up the booth." That did it. Hope told Dan, "I can't stand it any longer at my church; I want to try yours." The next Sunday, she went to Christ Church. She had visited Episcopal churches many times before, but this time she came to communion and made an appointment for later that week to speak with the rector.

She sat very erect in the chair, as she had learned to do in convent school when speaking with a priest: toward the front of the chair, back straight, both feet flat on the floor. Hope was not completely relaxed, to say the least, but she is never at a loss for words and she wanted to tell her story and ask dozens of questions about the Episcopal Church. An hour went by as she told me about the circumstances that had brought her to Christ Church on the previous Sunday, and finally she asked, "What should I do now?"

"I don't think you should do anything right now," I replied. "You've only come here once. You need to know a lot more about the Episcopal Church. So I think you should come for awhile and see what we're really like—and ask questions." There was a pause and a look of surprise and then she said, "That's what they never said over there."

For years afterwards I thought of that moment with Hope as summing up the difference in attitude between two kinds of Catholicism, as being exactly what any Episcopal priest should say and exactly how any interested Roman Catholic would respond. I thought I had said exactly the right thing and that the response was exactly right. Twenty years later, when Hope Adams had become my colleague, a priest of the Episcopal Church and rector of a parish in Connecticut, I reminded her of that moment. "And when I said to ask questions, was that what just you wanted to hear?"

"No," she replied. "I was really disappointed." She threw her arms wide: "I wanted you to say, 'WELCOME! Welcome home! We're glad you're here. Kneel down and let me bless you.' Instead, I felt as if I'd arrived and no one wanted me."

"Well," I said defensively, "suppose someone came in today and sat in your office and asked you that same question. What would you say?" There was, for a change, a pause in our conversation as Hope thought about it. "I guess," she finally acknowledged, "I would say, 'I don't think you should do anything right away, but keep coming to church and find out what we're really like—and ask questions.'"

However off-target I may have been at our first meeting, Christ Church was all she had hoped it would be. "Other places were stops along the way, but Christ Church was home. It fed my sense of mystery. The sermons refused to downsize it or explain it away. There was a wonderful sense of freedom and, for the first time, a sense of community. It wasn't just me and God. I didn't have to have all the answers myself, even the clergy didn't have to have all the answers, because the community had the answers. And I realized that a pilgrimage doesn't have to arrive: the kingdom is out there ahead of us and I don't have to find it enshrined right here."

Indeed, the kingdom had not arrived. Hope had found a church to help her along the journey, but there were still many painful turns along the way. Dan finished out the year in the guitar mass at St. Joseph's and then joined Hope at Christ Church. The following year, he played for a guitar mass at Christ Church. But his own demons were still driving him; he felt a need to get further from the city, out to the country. They moved to Wilton, Connecticut, two years later. It wasn't the country, just another suburb, but they didn't know it at the time. And it didn't solve Dan's problems either. Nor did the drinking.

Young couples, of course, seldom really know what a marriage relationship ought to be like. They have seen marriage only from the outside and being married is different from the inside. A new partner is different, too, from anyone they have known before. That's part of the attraction. So is it "normal" for a man to work hard and drink too much? Is living with the tensions that result simply one of those adjustments you have to make that they told you about in the Pre-Cana Conference?

Hope's way of coping was to do more and keep a good face on things. Now she has studied counseling and she knows the pattern is called "denial": "I controlled everything, fixed everything, got up earlier and worked harder—and facilitated his drinking." When Dan began talking about going to Alcoholics Anonymous, Hope saw no reason. Dan, an alcoholic? Of course not: he just drinks too much sometimes, it's nothing we can't work out. "My marriage was falling apart and I didn't know it."

Dan, on the other hand, knew something was wrong. He didn't like the Dan Adams he was seeing and he wanted to do something about it and reclaim his role in the family. He told Hope she was covering up, but "I need help and I'm going to get it." So he went to a meeting of AA, stopped drinking, and tried to take back some part of the family role Hope had taken on—which led to further conflict. Now Dan was threatening the image of herself Hope had created, trying to do the things she believed she did better than he. There was conflict also over the boys. Wilton in the 1970s was not Eden: Danny, the oldest boy, discovered marijuana in junior high. Dan let him smoke at home and Hope was horrified. It wasn't long before Dan found a female friend in AA who understood him better than his wife did.

Her marriage in chaos, Hope managed to find the first threads of a new pattern. She found a part-time job she loved as adjunct professor of physiology at Sacred Heart College in nearby Fairfield. The old interest in medicine, which had seemed to lead only to medical school, found expression in another way, in the give-and-take of teaching. Before long, Hope was teaching full-time and doing so well she was asked to write a textbook for wider use. But if being part of an academic community brought such a sense of fulfillment, she wondered if perhaps the lifelong sense of a vocation in the church could find expression in the work of a college chaplain. The call to ordination rose to the surface again in a new form: no longer the vision of a nun, but now, in the Episcopal Church, of a priest, a college chaplain, someone like that chaplain in Rochester who had been so willing to respond to her questions.

Few people would have the energy to stake out a new life in terms of family—maintaining a home for the boys without Dan's presence—while working as a college professor and adding the challenge of studying for ordination. For two years Hope did it all, commuting to New Haven to begin her work as a seminarian. Of course it was too much; after two years she gave up the teaching to attend seminary almost full-time.

Her vision of her ministry went through one more refinement. College chaplaincy is specialized, so the experience of a broader ministry is always useful. Hope decided to get some experience in an urban parish: Trinity Church, Hartford. And now, to her surprise, she really was home—here was the family, the community, she had been moving toward step by step, through so many apparent detours and reroutings for so many years. Here was a setting in which Hope could really be all God had been calling her to be.

Hope is now a priest whose experience includes a very full measure of what the Prayer Book calls "the changes and chances of this mortal life." Walk with her down the narrow streets of Essex and you see the police patrol car slow and give her a wave in passing. They know Hope as someone who works with them in a shared ministry of caring for a community with all its diverse needs and problems.

But if community is so important to her, what kind of community has she found in the Episcopal Church? In recent years it has become a community in turmoil, torn by interrelated tensions over sexuality, authority, liturgy, and budget. Hope takes it all in stride. "That's what families are like," she says. "A family argues over things like sex and money. We are a family, and these are the things we are arguing about this year."

In the midst of the adventure of life as she has known it, Hope has no facile answers about "God's plan": "I can understand how bits and pieces fit in—but it's too much to understand completely." Honesty and mystery are the two basic requirements. The Episcopal Church provides them both. "At least we aren't pretending to know the will of God with such precision," Hope will tell you; and now she leans back comfortably in her chair and feels free to cross her legs. "I've come to realize that my story is part of a larger story of pain and doubt and questioning. It's the story of God's people, the story of a God who challenges us and demands that we pay the price of growth."

"The price of growth" is a theme we will notice again in these stories. Change, as we have said, is seldom easy. Nor is there any one straight path to follow. There are many different roads that bring people into the Episcopal Church and sometimes the route seems more like a mysterious detour than a clearly marked highway. Hope Adams's story is one of quiet growth leading gradually to a moment when change could no longer be avoided. When that time came, she knew exactly where to go. For her—and this seems to be unusual—the discovery of the Episcopal Church had already occurred many years before. She needed to know much more, of course, but she already knew enough to enable her to come in and walk up the aisle to communion, confident that the gift of life would be there.

Jerry Lamb, on the other hand, had to turn away from the church that had nurtured him and only then, and after a long "vacation," find his way into a back pew where he could very slowly, with no one to push or pull, gain confidence that he was at last in the place where he belonged.

Have you heard the joke where one person says, "I don't believe in organized religion" and the other responds, "Neither do I—I'm an Episcopalian"? Jerry Lamb had not heard that joke in 1971 when he left the priesthood of the Roman Catholic Church. He loved being a priest but he had come to feel that the institutional church was a thing of the past and it was his firm intention to live the rest of his life without it. God, however, has a sense of humor. Over twenty years later, the man who had resolved to live his life without the institutional church is now a bishop.

Jerry remembers how, when he was growing up in Denver, there were ethnic neighborhoods and a parish for each neighborhood, each ethnic group. He grew up in a neighborhood that was overwhelmingly Roman Catholic, largely German, and centered on St. Elizabeth's Church. At one time St. Elizabeth's had been strictly a German-language parish, but when Jerry Lamb was a boy only the elderly still spoke German. The old ethnic neighborhoods were beginning to show signs of erosion. The bonds of language and culture were no longer a significant factor in uniting—and separating—people. As a result, Jerry lived in a larger world than his parents. Friendships were no longer controlled by the ethnic neighborhood. He had friends who went to St. Cajetan's in a Mexican neighborhood and other friends who went to St. Leo's in an Irish neighborhood. When he went with these friends, he recalls, "It was like visiting your uncle or aunt. It was the same family—but they did things a little differently."

The church as he knew it then was, indeed, like a family. His grandmother's involvement in the church included visiting those who were sick or dying, taking them meals, and doing errands as one would for a member of the family. He wonders, looking back, whether that had more to do with the ethnicity of the neighborhood than the teaching of the church, but it was all of a piece. The church made the neighborhood what it was and no one could imagine the one without the other.

Jerry went to parochial school as a matter of course, and when the nuns "found I behaved better if they gave me something to do," he became an acolyte. When that tactic succeeded, they continued to put opportunities to serve in front of him—and kept him behaving himself fairly well through grade school and the diocesan high school, Holy Family, run by the Sisters of Loretto. It was an easy and natural progression, a growing involvement in what amounted to an extended family, and the church was so central to it, so intimately involved in people's lives, that when the time came to go to college, Jerry Lamb had a very clear sense of direction. There were callings that had a certain appeal—the practice of medicine, the teaching profession—but priesthood seemed to offer the best combination of ways to serve others: to touch, to heal, to teach, to lift people up. He went off to St. Thomas' College to begin the long path of preparation for priesthood.

And it was, indeed, a long path. Four years of college with a major in philosophy and minors in history and education were followed by four years of seminary. The life of a seminarian was tightly disciplined and controlled; if you couldn't handle discipline in seminary, you might as well find it out, since you wouldn't be able to handle it as a parish priest either. Looking back, Jerry Lamb can acknowledge now that "it wasn't all that bad," but at the time he hated it: "I was being forced into a monastic life I knew I didn't want to live." Everything was regulated by lights and bells: time to get up, time to relax, time to study, time to go to bed. Meals were in common; all courses were prescribed without choice; attendance was taken four times a day; hair styles and length were regulated; cassocks were worn at all times except recreation. For students in the early sixties, it was a hard pattern of life to accept: Jerry Lamb's class started out with eighty-five seminarians, but only nineteen were ordained. Jerry Lamb was one of them. "I was willing to do it because I wanted to be a priest." In May of 1966, the nineteen survivors prostrated themselves on the floor of Denver's Cathedral of the Immaculate Conception and were ordained at last to the priesthood by the archbishop.

Perhaps the discipline and rigidity were made more endurable also by the vision of renewal—*aggiornamento*—held up by Pope John XXIII. His enthronement, and then the dramatic calling of the Second Vatican Council in the very year that Jerry Lamb started college, made it possible for Jerry to look forward to a time of serious and significant restructuring. He had no struggle about God or Jesus or the church; authority, as the church administered it, was the only important hurdle. It didn't have to change immediately or all at once, but it had to change. That much was clear. And now, with a pope who was talking about a new way of being the church, it seemed reasonable to hope that change could take place.

Jerry was excited by that hope. He read everything on the subject that he could get his hands on; he was ready to work to help build a new church for a new era. At the time he was ordained, the first signs of a slow metamorphosis were emerging. The translation of the Latin mass into English and the moving of altars out from the walls were the outward and visible evidence of change, a change that could be seen and heard every day in every church building. If these things, fixed and unshaken as they had been from time immemorial, could be changed, what more was possible? But John XXIII died, and it seemed to many that the vision died with him.

Meanwhile, Jerry was beginning to serve as a priest, working first for a year in All Saints' Church in South Denver with a pastor and one other assistant. There was all the normal work of the parish to be done, but Jerry had special responsibility for the children and young people. He must have done it well because the archbishop called after only a year to ask if he would be interested in becoming a college chaplain.

That was the era of Vietnam, an interesting time (to put it mildly) to be involved in college ministry. At Loretto Heights, a small church college with about twelve hundred students, Chaplain Lamb was responsible for a daily mass, regular retreats, counseling, and a variety of service ministries involving students with parishes in poorer neighborhoods. But there were also demonstrations against the war and the concerned chaplain spent endless hours trying to help the students think through their response to a war increasingly hard to understand or support.

Although they didn't know it, the students were not the only ones feeling frustrated by authority. Their chaplain, too, was growing impatient with a church so out of touch with the lives and events around him. Ask him if that frustration was intensified by the college setting and student unrest, and he will answer, "Oh, you betcha!" A parish priest in a blue-collar neighborhood might be able to go about his parish as if the world were not changing, but a college chaplain in touch with the students could hardly ignore it.

For Jerry, as for many others, the turning point was the issuance in 1968 of *Humanae Vitae*, the papal decree ruling out all artificial means of birth control. That was the moment when it seemed clear that nothing was going to change. What bothered him most was how unnecessary the decree was. The pope didn't need to say anything. He could simply have allowed a certain ambiguity to continue, but he chose instead to restate in the clearest possible terms that artificial means of birth control were prohibited. "How," Jerry Lamb asked himself, "do you preach eighty-five percent of an official position? What do you tell the couple struggling with the realities of their marriage?" And the larger question for Jerry Lamb was, "Can I continue to be a priest in a church like this?" It became increasingly clear he could not.

The struggle was finally resolved by what theologians sometimes call "non-theological factors." More specifically, Jerry met dorm supervisor Jane Onstad, a nurse who had "burned out" in the constant pressures and crises of that profession. She had come to Denver to get a bachelor's degree in English with the idea of becoming a teacher. As Jane had burned out in nursing, so Jerry had burned out in priesthood. Leaving that ministry had become simply a question of time—and Jane's presence helped determine the timing. Jane and Jerry decided to get married and Jerry let the archbishop know that he would be resigning his position.

The combination of marriage and priesthood was not a new idea to Jane; her father was an Episcopal priest. But it was not a combination that had any place in the current papal vision. Marriage for priests was unacceptable. So Jerry simply walked away. "I loved being a priest, but I felt the institutional church was a thing of the past. It wasn't that it was bad, just that it was useless." The young couple moved to Eugene, Oregon, where the University of Oregon offered a program in counseling and Jerry Lamb found a job selling plumbing and electrical supplies for a well-known chain of stores in the area, while studying part-time.

As for Jane and her church, that was her business. Jerry agreed to go to her church for the wedding because it was her father, of course, who was going to do it. But the institutional church—especially one of the Protestant churches—had no place in his new plan of life. He liked his new father-in-law, but he knew very well that the Episcopal Church was just one more Protestant sect and irrelevant to his needs and plans. He had been brought up, like so many Roman Catholics, to believe that there was only one church and if that church was beyond hope, there was really no other.

This assumption was still in force at the wedding rehearsal, where Jane's father had the new experience of being told how to do things by the groom: "It was the first time," he told Jerry afterwards, "I've ever listened to a groom about anything." Later Jerry would also listen to his father-in-law, but not yet. The long years of narrow discipline had left him in need of a healing space. On Sundays, when Jane went to church, Jerry went fishing. She could do her thing and he could do his—and his had no more room for a church.

A new marriage and family and job, combined with part-time studies, does not, of course, leave much time for anything else anyway. Nor was life much simpler when the degree was finally completed and Jerry went to work for the State of Oregon as a parole officer, a job that involved keeping tabs on rapists and drug addicts—the sorts of people Jesus would probably have been more comfortable with than most clergy. Jerry got to know the back streets and bars of Eugene, Oregon, places where parole officers were not very welcome and where someone with a gun might always be waiting for you. There were also, of course, the individuals who had made one mistake and could be helped to get their lives straightened out. The satisfaction of being able to do that occasionally made the job worthwhile.

But life on the streets very quickly began to take its toll. Jerry Lamb was learning the hard way how vital a Christian community can be. "I realized," he reflects, "that I needed that balance in my life. Without a community of my own, I was going to become part of the community I was dealing with. You take on the lifestyle and attitudes of people around you. Ask any police officer; they'll tell you how quickly your values are corrupted by the values of those you're dealing with."

Unlike most of those he was dealing with, Jerry Lamb knew what a community with strong values could do for you. And now he also knew that there was a Christian community other than the Roman Catholic Church that might be what he needed. Also, by a nice coincidence, he was in close personal contact with one of its members! In fact, there was even a priest of that church who was his father-in-law and with whom there had by now been opportunity for a number of long conversations. And did his father-in-law push books at him? "No, he never pushed anything at me; that would have been counterproductive. People let me find my own way. But Jane had books and stuff lying around and I would pick them up."

Episcopalians often worry about their lack of an aggressive evangelistic style, but sometimes the best evangelism is so low-key as to be invisible. Sometimes the Spirit is able to work most effectively in human lives if the church's agents stay out of the way. Looking back, Jerry Lamb believes that the Spirit had been leading him toward the Episcopal Church for a very long time. He will tell you, in fact, that he "became an Anglican my first year in seminary when I said that the pope is a nice man and we all need leaders, but as an absolute authority, he isn't necessary. And that came out of my family, who were always rebels. I'd been raised to think. I was never forced to accept something."

So walking into St. Mary's Church in Eugene, Oregon, was really just the next step on a journey that had started long before. It was a slow and cautious step, but the right one. St. Mary's was Jane's church and Jerry began going to the 8 a.m. service with her. Again, nobody pushed. For four or five months, he went quietly to the early service until he began to feel comfortable enough to have a conversation with the rector. The conversation went well, and Jerry began to meet a larger group of Episcopal clergy. Serving with the rector at St. Mary's was a group of clergy, both paid and non-stipendiary, who could take the new-comer on his own terms, who could wait until he asked and then give him what he asked for.

They didn't have to wait long. Jerry, after all, had been ordained a priest because he had a vocation and now that vocation could begin to assert itself more strongly than ever. The newcomer had certain gifts and he began exploring ways he could be helpful in the parish, maybe helping out a bit with adult education, maybe working with families where there were problems with drugs or with the law. He had no clearly formulated ideas as yet about the shape his ministry might take, but there did seem to be some ways in which he could be useful.

He was, indeed, useful, and it began to seem strange that the priest who played so valuable a role in people's lives couldn't really function as a priest; that critical element was missing in his ministry. So a conversation began with the Bishop of Oregon, Matthew Bigliardi, about the process of being accepted as a priest of the Episcopal Church. The bishop was encouraging, and a plan was formed for Jerry Lamb to continue to be a parole officer and to contribute his skills to the church on an unpaid basis. He was never to be in charge of a congregation: that, after all, still seemed a little too much like the institutional church he had written off as hopeless. But "never" is a category the Holy Spirit doesn't always respect, especially when it conflicts with the Spirit's agenda. As Jerry Lamb became more deeply involved in parish life it began to seem that the Episcopal Church was really home and, if it was home, maybe it wouldn't be that bad after all to go back into parish ministry on a full-time basis.

As it happened, there was a church in Coos Bay, about seventy-five miles from Eugene, where an assistant priest was needed. Coos Bay, as Jerry remembers it, was a "terrific" parish. There were two full-time priests and a director of Christian education. Jerry was asked to take a full share of parish ministry, especially of course with the young people with whom he had so much experience and so much rapport. Inevitably, it wasn't long before the opportunity came to take on a still larger responsibility. A call came from Trinity Church, Ashland, in the southwest corner of the state, almost on the California border, a region of such scenic beauty that even now Jerry goes into rhapsodies about it at the least opportunity: "One of those wonderful spots that God designs just once in a while." There's a college in town, Southern Oregon State, and the oldest Shakespeare Festival in the west. What better place to settle in and use the gift of priesthood and serve a community and raise a family? Clearly, Jerry Lamb would be hard put to imagine such a place.

The problem, of course, is that even in a distant corner of the state it is hard to do well in a medium-sized diocese without being noticed. The Lambs had been in Ashland only five years when a process of change began in the diocese. A bishop coadjutor, Robert Ladehoff, was called from North Carolina in 1985 to begin learning about the diocese so he could take over leadership when Bishop Bigliardi retired. Three years later, Bishop Bigliardi retired and the diocese had a new chief pastor. One thing Bishop Ladehoff had learned as he traveled around the diocese was that there was a very competent priest in Ashland who might be exactly the person he needed to assist him in his new ministry. And so the man who had walked away from the institutional church found himself working full-time in a diocesan office.

It was, he will tell you in self-defense, very much a "people job." He was working with candidates for ordination and parishes looking for a new priest. The bishop had also been on the job long enough to recognize that the bishop, chief pastor though he may be, cannot always be a pastor to his clergy. The bishop is also the chief executive to whom the other clergy report, and that fits poorly with the work of pastoring. Understanding this, the bishop wanted someone working with him who could be a pastor to those who couldn't confide in the bishop.

Jerry Lamb, he discovered, was exactly right for that ministry. A background as a probation officer may not seem like good training to be a pastor to pastors, but in some ways it couldn't be more apt. When clergy misconduct cases came along, the new assistant would wade right in. "He didn't put up with any nonsense from people," Bishop Ladehoff reports, "yet everybody liked him. So much so that he could step on toes and get away with it. He was perceived as altogether fair, and it was obvious that he cared deeply about people. He had a great gift for coming in and saying 'This is what we're going to do.'" This gift for getting on with the job meant Jerry Lamb could do a lot and "make it look easy."

So there he was, at the center of the institution—and fitting in so well that others began to notice. Just to the south, only a few miles from Ashland, the diocese of Northern California was beginning to look for a new bishop. Someone suggested they might not have to search very far, that there was a priest in the diocesan office just north of them who might have exactly the gifts they hoped to find.

But who would want to be a bishop? It's often seen as the supreme example of the institutional church, and certainly it puts the problems of the institutional church on the desk of the man or woman who sits there and who comes to the position most often from a parish where pastoral issues have been the priority. There is always a tension between what the church wants a bishop to be and what it requires a bishop to do. One senior bishop has suggested that anyone nominated for the job should accept the nomination and, if elected, should accept the election, be consecrated, send the pictures home to mother—and then resign.

Bishop Lamb doesn't see it that way. Northern California, he believes, is a diocese of "just the right size": the small parish communities and fewer than seventy priests make it possible for a bishop to be a pastor. The one "horrible problem" he sees is the terrific distances involved: some members of the diocese have to drive as much as three hundred and sixty miles to attend diocesan events. Technology, the cellular phone in particular, helps overcome the distance, since the bishop can keep in touch from his car as he travels.

The long drives also provide opportunity for reflection on the way Christians live together in the Episcopal Church. The responsibility taken by the laity has been the biggest discovery for Bishop Lamb. "I expected it," he says, "and it's not that it threw me for a loop, but it still takes some getting used to. I was an autocrat in my own little way and I would say, 'We're going to do this,' and I'd get an 'Oh, yeah?' That's not the way priests responded to bishops in the church where I grew up!"

That freedom to question is, however, not so much a cause of division as the source of unity. The priests and people of the diocese of Northern California have very different visions of what the church should be, but they are willing to be open with each other about it and make clear where they stand. "I do think," says Jerry Lamb, "that we have people envisioning the church in distinct and separate ways. Some see it as a once-for-all proposition, while others see it as continually changing and adapting. I think there's a core doctrine that's absolute and unchanging, but around that a lot can change, including some things we once taught as absolutes."

The vision Bishop Lamb holds up for the people of Northern California is closely related to his experience of the church as he grew up in the ethnic neighborhoods of Denver. He uses the image of extended family, clan, and tribe to evoke a sense of the unity without which the diocese might be only a loose confederation of churches in some kind of geographical proximity. The bishop is also clear, however, that the church today cannot function as simply as parishes did when he was growing up, because too much has changed in the past fifty years: "The things that you and I came to know and to expect from a community when we were growing up as children in the church may not be an appropriate way for us to function as God's people at this time. The world is a vastly different place."

What, then, gives the church its unity? "Is there," Bishop Lamb asked in speaking to his first clergy conference, "a central authority—or are we all going off in multiple directions with no commonality and very little relationship one to another?" It is, perhaps, the central question of Anglican existence and one that a former Roman Catholic may have a better perspective on than someone raised in the Episcopal Church. Bishop Lamb's answer is that "we have historic roots in the One Holy Catholic and Apostolic Church" and we find our unity in "a strange blend that is always in tension" between those roots in tradition and the roots that go "deep in the Reformation experience about the rights and freedom of the individual." That tension between freedom and authority can't always provide clear answers and direction, but it may offer a better way to respond to the world.

It was an institutional church that seemed to lack that ability to respond that Jerry Lamb left behind, and he has no intention of allowing the churches in his diocese to lapse into a similar irrelevance. "Are we even dealing with the questions that people are asking at this time?" he asked his first diocesan convention. "Or are we so 'ivory-towered' that we are missing the reality of the world around us?" Jerry Lamb's brief experience of being a bishop has been "life-changing" for him, has made him more aware of the gifts the institutional church possesses, as well as the "plight of the poor of the world." "We must go out into the world," he told his diocese, "being renewed, supported, and nurtured by our Christian communities."

In that journey, as Bishop Ladehoff noted in his sermon at Jerry Lamb's consecration, the diocese of Northern California has appropriate leadership: "Today, a Lamb becomes a Shepherd. A servant bishop for a servant people."

So here we have two journeys that led into the Episcopal Church. Most new Episcopalians will not become bishops or priests, but perhaps it's good to start with these two stories because they make it clear that even those who were subsequently given leadership roles in the church were fearful about coming in.

It is painful, first of all, to realize that the church you belong to, in which you were baptized and nurtured, cannot meet your needs anymore. Whether the initiative comes from the individual or from the church, it seems like rejection and that is never easy to accept. Furthermore, if you have been hurt in one relationship, it is harder to form another and risk being hurt again. It may be easier to go fishing than to take the chance of another wound. However much you may be drawn to someone else or to another church, how can you be sure that this new relationship will provide real understanding? If you reveal yourself completely, will you be understood or rejected?

For a long time after she became an Episcopalian, Hope Adams kept very quiet about her background. There was still the fear that something important to her might be scorned and rejected by someone in her new church. Indeed, she has found over the years that some of the old bitterness toward Rome is still present: when someone exclaims, "Oh, I didn't know you had been a *Roman Catholic*!" the implied message sometimes is, "I didn't know you had been one of *them*, with all their superstitions and idolatries." That reaction can still hurt people who feel that they have much to be grateful for in their Roman Catholic background, who believe that they found gifts there they might not have found had they grown up in the Episcopal Church.

Changing church membership is seldom a decision that we can make alone. We may well have parents who brought us up carefully in their church and would see a change as a rejection not simply of their faith but of themselves. Church membership is often tightly bound up with family loyalty and ethnic identity.

When you talk to Roman Catholics today, they will often tell you, "My parents were Irish" or "My father was Italian but my mother was Polish." But they seldom say, "I am Irish" or "I am Polish-Italian." For their parents' generation, the ethnic identification was still vitally important; for the current generation—except among people of Hispanic background, a newer generation of immigrants—the ethnic identification is more of a memory than a living fact. For their parents to leave the Roman Catholic Church was almost unimaginable: being Irish or Italian or Polish or German included being Roman Catholic. To change your church was to change your total identity, and few people were brave enough to do it. Those who did often faced pressure from their families that we can hardly imagine.

For Roman Catholics especially, coming as most of them did from non-English backgrounds, the church and their ethnic identity enabled them to survive in a new and foreign world. But today that is seldom a factor and most Roman Catholics think of themselves as Americans first of all, whether their names begin or end with an O. Church membership is no longer so closely connected with ethnic identity; because membership is worn more lightly, it is easier to change when we are dissatisfied. And many American Christians *are* dissatisfied. We have all seen the bumper sticker that says, "Question authority!" We are taught to ask questions and when the church we go to doesn't give us good answers, we are very likely to begin looking around for one that does.

Coming into a new church, it may seem as if there is a rectangle in the path ahead that may open up and swallow you. Hope Adams walked across it and it held her up. Jerry Lamb went fishing for awhile and then knelt for months in a back pew before moving forward. Coming in may not be easy, but if we are able to find a community based on something deeper than ethnicity, a family that can face fears and doubts and questions honestly, where the members are able to support each other, in which the gifts we bring are respected and valued, then the journey may be worth the risk.

2

Finding Home

Teresa Gordon and Colleen Sica

"I knew I was home." *(Teresa Gordon)*

"Everything they had taken away from me as a little girl was there: mystery, transcendence, liturgy, poetry. I'd been away from Rome my whole adult life, but I knew what this was and where it came from. I never left or tried anything else. I was home." *(Colleen Sica)*

Just east of Times Square in New York City, on a street lined with small restaurants, music shops, and rundown offices, stands a great gray Gothic building with a sign that reads "The Church of St. Mary the Virgin" and lists the times of daily and Sunday masses. It happens to be an Episcopal church, but there is no outward evidence of that. In the days when the Roman Catholic mass was still in Latin, Roman Catholics in the area would occasionally wander in at the time for mass, see the statues and votive lights and confessionals, and assume they were in a Roman Catholic church. So they would kneel quietly in the back of the church, watching the priests at the distant altar, and, because they expected that the priest would be speaking Latin and therefore made no effort to hear what was said, they never noticed that the priests were, in fact, speaking English and that they were not in a Roman Catholic church. Today, when the eucharist in both churches is ordinarily in English, it would be even harder to tell the difference.

Teresa Gordon, however, was hoping to find a difference when she walked into Trinity on the Hill, in Los Alamos, New Mexico—and she did. Let her tell the story in her own words: "I walked into the church on Sunday morning, the second Sunday in Advent, and there on the altar was a vested chalice and flowers. The vessels on the credence table were silver, not ugly ceramic. I started to cry from happiness immediately. There were kneelers in the pews. More tears of happiness. The choir, in robes, processed in with the lay ministers, also in robes, and flags. Obviously, these people believed in giving God their best in worship.

"I don't remember what the entrance hymn was, but it was worth singing, all four or five or however many verses there were of it. Fr. Kelly began, 'Almighty God, to whom all hearts are open, all desires known....' Here was a prayer worth praying. We sang the *Kyrie*. We read a substantial portion of a psalm. There was a real gospel procession with another hymn worth singing. The prayers of the people had a real content—the whole Anglican communion, let alone the local parish, seemed to truly care for those for whom they prayed. We sang the doxology at the offertory. Fr. Kelly sang the preface. We all prayed, 'And here we offer and present unto Thee our selves, our souls and bodies....'

"I received communion with the reminder that this was 'the body of Christ which was given for thee.' An hour and a half later I was regretting that the service was over. Boy, what a switch that was. Always before if the service went much over half an hour, all I could think was how much of my time was being wasted. Needless to say, I knew I was home."

"I knew I was home." It's interesting to notice how often former Roman Catholics in the Episcopal Church describe their change of church membership that way. But what makes a church "home"? How can a new and different church be more like home than the one to which you have always belonged? Clearly two factors are at work. In the first place, to leave one church for another, there must be something going on that makes the first church no longer feel like "home," no longer fit our expectations of what a church should be. But second, there must be something deeply ingrained in our background experience of the church, something which has been valued and which we still hope to find. In leaving the church we grew up in, we are not looking for something different, but something the same. Teresa Gordon speaks of hymns "worth singing," prayers with "real content," and a sense that Episcopalians were "giving God their best." Her background in the Roman Catholic Church had led her to value such things. She valued them enough to go looking for them elsewhere when she could not find them where she was. And when she found them, she felt that she had come home.

When Colleen Sica walked into Christ Church, Bronxville, for the first time, her feelings were very much the same: "It was a jewel of a church," she recalls, "with perfect acoustics, an amazing organ, and an ethereal choir singing gorgeous music, prayers that sounded like poetry, and a good sermon. Everything they had taken away from me as a little girl was there: mystery, transcendence, liturgy, poetry. I'd been away from Rome my whole adult life, but I knew what this was and where it came from. I never left or tried anything else. I was home."

Home is where things are familiar: not just the shape of the building and the way it is furnished, but the moves people make in that setting, the way they act and the way they talk. Young people can get accustomed to a college dorm, but it never really becomes home. A newly married couple can have a place of their own but still talk about going home, his or hers, for Thanksgiving and Christmas. Even if their parents retire and move away from the home where the children grew up, they can still "go home" because their parents will talk the same way and act the same way, wherever they happen to live. They will gather at the table in the same way and find there the same turkey with the same kind of cranberry sauce and the same pecan or pumpkin pie at the end of the meal. The building may be different but it will still be home because every family has its own liturgy and children brought up with that liturgy will always identify it as "home."

In the same way, Roman Catholics—at least those brought up in the church prior to the mid-1960s—have usually been brought up with deep feelings about liturgy and music. The way priests and acolytes move at the altar, the words and music, the sense of awe—all these shape the expectations with which they come to worship. When those expectations are not met, a certain discomfort develops, and when they are met, it feels like being "home." Neither Teresa Gordon nor Colleen Sica left the Roman Catholic Church because the liturgy had changed; it was one factor among many and probably not the most important. But when they went looking for a church where they could be at home, it was liturgy and music that told them they had arrived at a place where they could be comfortable, where the sounds and the movements were part of a pattern they already knew. Indeed, they might feel that the new church was more like home than home itself if the liturgy were performed with even greater care and reverence.

A sense of home obviously begins very early in life. Teresa Gordon has vivid and detailed memories of the magnificence of St. Joseph's Church in Shawnee, Kansas, just outside Kansas City. The church of her childhood had been built by the parishioners themselves, including one of her uncles, out of native limestone. She can still describe in detail the altar with its carved *Alpha* and *Omega* painted in gold and its red-violet dossal and canopy, the marble side altars, and the statues of the Virgin, St. Joseph, St. Agnes, and St. Lucy. St. Lucy, she remembers, was holding a dish with a pair of eyeballs on it. Stained glass windows portrayed the mysteries of the rosary. It was, as she remembers it, "an elegant, beautiful place, full of awe and wonder...an edifice worthy of a real God."

The ceremonies inside the church were "elegant and awesome" as well: solemn processions involving the parochial school children, "smells and bells," and Gregorian chant drifting down from a choirloft high at the west end of the church. A special adventure was climbing up the long flights of wooden stairs to be with her parents when they sang in the choir. Even St. Lucy's eyeballs, in their own exotic way, conveyed a sense of mystery, something beyond the logical streets of a town in Kansas. Trinity on the Hill lacked the statuary and the choirloft at the back of the church, but the particular furniture was not the essence of it so much as the atmosphere of reverence, the feeling of beauty and mystery engendered by everything that was done.

For Colleen, above all, it was the music. Music was a part of her parochial school experience from the very beginning. The children began to learn plainsong in first grade and Colleen had a good ear and a good voice. In fifth grade, when the nuns needed someone to play the organ for school services, Colleen was the obvious choice. She loved it. Now she got to skip the regular music classes, which were dull, to practice the organ alone in an empty church. Music was the royal road to happiness, and God was calling Colleen down that road.

In all the stories in this book, liturgy and music are among the most important qualities that speak of home. But we should tell the whole story to see how these elements are woven into a larger picture.

"If I could have tailored a church to fit my own individual specifications," says Teresa Gordon, "it would be the Episcopal Church. It is truly the answer to my prayers."

But who on earth could tailor a church to meet Teresa Gordon's specifications? Take, for example, these elements: a love of science, especially astronomy; an instinctive dislike of the Bible; a great respect for the Episcopal Church's current *enfant terrible*, Bishop Spong; a negative attitude toward peace-niks and political correctness; a love of the 1979 Prayer Book, especially Rite I; a dislike for "psychobabble" and "touchy-feelies"; a deep belief in prayer; a love of good music and strong, traditional hymns; and a long commitment to tithing. It would be hard to imagine one person combining these traits, let alone a church. Where would you begin?

In Teresa Gordon's case, you would need to begin in Shawnee, Kansas, just outside Kansas City, with a sensitive, Roman Catholic child. Growing up sensitive in Kansas is much the same as growing up anywhere else in the world with a feeling that children elsewhere are smarter or better looking or better at games, or all the above. Very often it isn't true and the truth will emerge eventually, but meanwhile it leads the child to look for an area of life in which to excel, which is special for him or her.

For Teresa Gordon, life was about as perfect as it could be until she started first grade. The household into which she was born included her father, in his forties, and her mother, age thirty-nine, an eighteen-year-old half-sister, and a grandmother. Admiration of the youngest member of the family was not in short supply. But then, suddenly, at the age of six, without benefit of kindergarten or other preparation, she was plunged into a parochial school classroom containing sixty children (first and second graders together) with one teacher. Simultaneously, a new little brother arrived to usurp her central place in the family. Teresa felt "dethroned, exiled, and generally unappreciated."

It made things worse that she didn't enjoy studying history, arithmetic, or the Bible, and that when recess time came they played baseball, for which she believed she had less aptitude than Charlie Brown in *Peanuts*. Parochial school got off to a bad start and the negative memories still seem to outweigh the positive. One "really bad memory" came from seventh grade, when Teresa's classmates discovered that she had a powerful fear of snakes and that there was a double-paged spread of colored pictures of snakes in the *Encyclopedia Britannica Junior*. Displaying the picture of snakes to tease Teresa became a popular sport that year. A broken relationship with the Almighty is the reason given for Eve's antipathy to snakes, but in Teresa Gordon's case, snakes helped build a deeper relationship with God. The nuns had taught her to turn to prayer in time of difficulty, and the pictures of snakes drove her constantly to prayer.

Radical changes came after Teresa graduated from eighth grade and her parents moved to a farm thirty miles from Kansas City. Holy Family Church, in the small town of Eudora, was a tiny building with no side altars or marble floors, but the priest was kind and the mass was still the same with its incense and bells and Gregorian chant. So small a church, on the other hand, could hardly maintain a parochial high school, so now Teresa would be going to public school. And to that school she would bring two late discoveries from the parochial school: a great love of the math she had once hated and a fascination with astronomy.

Astronomy, with its vision of vast and empty spaces, opened up "the possibility that somewhere in this unbelievably enormous universe there was another creature just as lonely and persecuted as I." Besides, in all the rest of that vast expanse, there were no snakes! As for the changed attitude toward math, that came when the class was introduced to geometry, and suddenly everything was turned around: now Teresa was in her element and the children who had excelled in arithmetic before were at a loss. On her placement test for high school she scored one hundred percent in math and was recognized as the star of the class. It didn't do much for her popularity with her classmates, but "the teachers thought I was splendid, and that was enough for me."

But what becomes of a young woman from a Kansas farm when high school is over and funds for college are scarce? Career counseling and college entrance guidance were ideas whose time had not yet come, and those like Teresa who were not inclined to go back to the farm were left to flounder. Nursing school was the first idea she had for a next step, but only a week of that made Teresa aware of how much she would miss the math and astronomy. A small Benedictine college was a second idea but she knew by then that anyone interested in astronomy needed physics and for one whole academic year she was repeatedly told that "girls don't major in physics!"

The third idea was the University of Kansas, only ten miles away. Not only did the university have physics and chemistry and math, they had seen Teresa's high school transcripts and so they put her in advanced sections. But while Teresa had been starring in a rural high school and struggling with a small college that wouldn't or couldn't offer the challenge she wanted in science or math, her classmates had been doing real science and advanced math in the big cities of Lawrence, Topeka, and Kansas City. Not only that, the advanced sections were also full of older students, veterans coming back from the Korean War who had taken various technical courses in the service. Teresa Gordon had never had to work before to learn anything; learning had been easy and natural. Now, for the first time, she had to work hard to catch up and keep up.

College years, of course, are often a time when childhood faith is reevaluated: modified, deepened, or abandoned. The late 1950s were, additionally, a challenging time for Roman Catholics because there was a new pope; an ecumenical council had been summoned and the winds of change were beginning to blow. For Teresa Gordon, living at home and commuting to college, the familial routine of frequent evening devotions and biweekly confession was beginning to be more of an irritant than a source of strength. In particular, she was beginning to feel that the regular presentation of "the usual laundry list of sins" at confession simply to keep the priest satisfied was not, to put it mildly, a valuable means of spiritual renewal. College studies brought her into contact also with thinkers like Martin Luther, George Orwell, Rene Descartes, and Bertrand Russell. Luther, in particular, was disturbing; his arguments "rang a bit too true for me to dismiss."

But Teresa Gordon's faith in God was not shaken by all of this. When a book on the philosophy of science stated pointblank that anyone who was afraid to study science for fear it would challenge their God didn't have much of a God to begin with, she agreed entirely. Her fascination with physics and astronomy was derived in large part from the fact that they revealed so incomprehensibly huge a universe, and the greater the universe, the greater the God must be who created it. What she was not sure of any longer was whether the Roman Church fully shared her faith. Pope John XXIII's call for reform made good sense and raised her hopes.

Meanwhile, among the members of her advanced physics class for seniors Teresa had noticed from afar an older, more brilliant student named James Wylie Gordon. Through the random pairing of lab partners, they began working together in the laboratory. In the close proximity of this partnership, she decided that he was the man she would marry. Such decisions, of course, need to be communicated to both persons involved, and there was no opportunity for Teresa to let Jim know of her decision. Nothing daunted, at the end of her senior year she decided to sign up for graduate school in the hope that Jim would be there. The long summer came to an end, and there he was. Teresa let him in on her plans, and after that, as Jim remembers it, "it was all downhill." Soon they were planning their wedding.

Jim Gordon, as it happened, was an Episcopalian, but that seemed like a very minor obstacle. It was clear to both that the churches had a lot in common and, with Vatican II in full swing, it seemed reasonable to hope that the two churches would be reunited before long anyway. They couldn't have a nuptial mass or enter the sanctuary but they could be married in the church. (Some years earlier, Teresa's aunt and her husband had had to be married in the priest's office, so progress was obviously being made.) The wedding took place and the new couple settled into a graduate student apartment to complete their programs, with a Ph.D. for him and a master's degree for her.

For a while they kept going to separate churches but, when they moved to Colorado Springs so Jim could begin work with Kaman Sciences and found that neither of their churches was within walking distance, it seemed better for Jim to join Teresa's church. He thought it would be better for the growing family—one child born just over a year after the wedding and another two years after that—to have one church in common. English would soon be the language of both churches anyway, and Jim's bottom-line requirement of any church was simply that it not intrude on his relationship with God. The priest conducting the inquirers' class, like the priest who performed their marriage, was friendly and intelligent, and the liturgy was familiar, though lacking, he said, "the eloquence and grandeur of the 1928 *Book of Common Prayer.*"

There were, however, some problems lurking in both their relationship with each other and with the church. The young couple's relationship with each other was shadowed by what seemed at the time to be a minor and not overwhelming problem: Jim was diagnosed with *ankylosing spondylitis*, arthritis of the spine. The Ben Gay that Teresa had been rubbing into his lower back since before they were married was obviously not the solution; indomethacin was substituted and medical science seemed to have triumphed. It would be many years before they realized that the indomethacin had been gradually leading to a chronic depression that might well have destroyed their marriage.

As for the young couple's relationship with the church, that was affected negatively when the arrival of the third child in five years brought the church's stand on birth control into a new and more immediate focus. Teresa's Roman Catholic doctor told her he himself saw nothing wrong with artificial birth control; his authority was not theoretically greater than the pope's, but it seemed more helpful so they accepted it.

But now there was a feeling of guilt, which only increased when the Vietnam war gave rise to a strong peace movement in the church, a movement that seemed to have gained the blessing of the hierarchy. Jim was hard at work designing nuclear warheads for submarine-launched ballistic missiles, so now the Gordons felt like sinners both in their work and in their personal lives. It didn't help that, at this critical time, the mass was at last being said in English and the hoped-for moment turned out to be a bitter disappointment. Gone were the awe and the mystery. In Teresa's view the God she had studied and admired, the Creator of the universe, had been demoted to chairman of the committee.

The situation was not improved by a move to New Mexico so Jim could work at the Los Alamos National Laboratory. Teresa's hope that a parish in a predominantly scientific community might have good music was quickly disappointed. Her early exposure to Gregorian chant left her with an instinctive feel for good music. While still in graduate school she joined the choir and the reform process had enabled them to sing both Martin Luther's great hymn "A mighty fortress is our God" and the Anglican doxology "Praise God from whom all blessings flow." Now, however, the reform process had moved on to guitars and folk masses with lyrics like "Happy the man who has a burning goal. . . . This man has found his own soul" and "Run with your head up in the wind" and "Eat his body, drink his blood, and we'll sing a song of love." The last of these made her think of cannibals at an orgy. She joined a committee at her parish, the Immaculate Heart of Mary, to help pick hymns, but one vote for the great hymns was not enough and she came away only feeling defeated.

Two years after the move to Los Alamos the parish distributed a questionnaire to ask, "What do you like/not like about Immaculate Heart of Mary?" Teresa was ready with some answers: "What don't I like about IHM? Hoo, boy, you asked for it, and you're finally going to get it. Where do I start?" A long-seething anger finally began to boil over. The sermons, the hymns, the lack of direction and purpose, the low standards of giving (the Gordons were tithing their gross income and knew something about what was possible): all were fuel for the fire.

But at the center of her frustration was a need for one thing only: "There is no one in this parish calling us to a closer, more intimate relationship with God. The entire emphasis of this parish seems to be on what we can do for each other rather than on what God has done and will continue to do for us." Why, she wanted to know, can't we have sermons about the Trinity and the Incarnation, the lives of the saints, the thoughts of Teilhard de Chardin, Thomas Aquinas, or any number of other great thinkers of the church, or the great heritage of the Catholic Church, or doctrines like Purgatory and the Communion of Saints? "Those are beliefs that make darn good sense...[but] all I've heard for many years past now is modern psychology and the Law." If there was a reply, Teresa doesn't remember it.

Complicating the whole matter was a rather rapid rotation of clerical leadership. The pastor whose sermons seemed to come from *Psychology Today* was succeeded by one who assembled a group to produce a statement on "Nuclear Weapons and Morality: A View from Los Alamos," which was helpful, and then by two more pastors in rapid succession. The Gordons were distressed when pastors continued to disappear suddenly and without explanation. Their protests brought a meeting with a deacon who told them that allegations of misconduct were behind some of the changes in leadership—which made the Gordons wonder further about a church which would deal with such allegations by transferring clergy from one parish to another.

Teresa's approach to problems in the parish had always been to get more involved: if you don't like the hymns, get on the committee. If the preaching doesn't help, join a Bible study group. She associated herself with a charismatic group in the parish, hoping to work with them toward a deeper faith.

The charismatics emphasized reading the Bible, so she decided to try it. What a shock! Here, instead of the Creator of the universe, was "a petty little arbitrary despot." No wonder, she thought to herself, the Roman Church had never encouraged people to read the Bible independently; they really knew what they were doing. But now she had a choice: abandon her God or jettison the Bible. So the Bible had to go, and with it the charismatics. Indeed, the church almost went, too, since the whole picture of a chosen people in the Bible was so unflattering and the Roman Church had always presented itself as God's chosen people.

But, however much Teresa might be tempted to let the Bible and the church go, God would not let her go. She remembers a summer day during her time with the charismatics when, as she was picking strawberries and feeling sorry for herself, she felt God suggesting that if she were indeed beyond his care, she would not have been given such good strawberries. "Aw," she said, "you give everybody strawberries." "No, I don't," was the reply, and she had to admit it was true.

And then there was the time when she was crying bitterly over something long forgotten and asked God what she had done to deserve wading through such muck. "You have asked to be my friend," was the reply, "and to help me in whatever small way you can. Well, this is what happens to my friends." Put that way, she could only feel privileged to help Christ carry the cross.

The burden might have been less if the Gordons' own relation-ship had been better. For years, it seemed to Teresa, Jim was increasingly critical of almost everything she did. He didn't like her clothes or the way the kids behaved or the way she yelled at them. He seemed to do nothing much around the house except read and watch television. Finally Teresa called Jim's doctor and asked whether the arthritis medicine might be affecting him. Yes, said the doctor, it might. Not without considerable grumbling, Jim agreed to try other medications. It helped, but the symptoms continued to return and still, over time, to worsen.

Now it was Teresa's turn to look for help. A psychiatrist referred her to the Family Council, where a counselor suggested she get a job outside the home. That helped in some ways, but home life deteriorated further. A switch to part-time helped more; it left time for home and family while enabling her to use some of her education and find support from her work group as well.

Finally, in 1987, the slow-building agony reached a critical turning point. In July of that year, Jim was honored by the Department of Energy with its E. O. Lawrence Memorial Award for "his outstanding innovations in the design and development of nuclear weapons with tailored effects and for his broad achievements in nuclear weapons effects, and vulnerability." Such an award should have been a great morale builder but, oddly enough, it wasn't. Instead, Jim found himself losing confidence in himself very gradually and subtly. He tells the story this way: "It was as though I were grading myself on everything I did. 'Humph. You get a C for that one.' I began to have considerable trouble sleeping. I had no idea what might be wrong or what to do about it. Finally, one morning I cried out to God that I couldn't stand it any longer, please help. And he did help, in probably the only way that would have gotten me the help I needed. That very day it blew up in my face in a way that forced me to get professional help then and there, first for the immediate problem and then for the long-term solution, which after a year and a half of medication and therapy was successful. Was God with me through all of this, and other crises in my life? You bet. 'I lift up my eyes unto the hills. From whence cometh my help? My help cometh from the Lord who made heaven and earth.'"

And now, thought Teresa Gordon, I can get my church back, too. Through thick and thin, they had stuck with the church. Discouraged by the preaching, the music, the parochial school their children attended, the lack of consistent leadership, she had run out of reasons for continuing except that Jim insisted. But there was new hope at home and a new pastor at the church, so she made an appointment with the priest to see what might be done. Unfortunately, he was not helpful. It seemed to Teresa that she was "ready to spit nails" and the pastor hardly cared. Finally he asked her what she thought the purpose of the church might be. "It's to draw people closer to God," she replied. "No," said the priest with more fervor than he had shown through the whole hour-long conversation. "The purpose of the church is to tell people what God wants them to do."

Teresa was halfway home before she fully realized what she had been told. Her first reaction had been that the priest was agreeing with her, restating her definition in his own words, but then it dawned on her that they were not in agreement at all. Now, at last, it was time to look at alternatives. It seemed to Jim and Teresa, as they talked it over, that the only real alternatives were the Lutheran Church and the Episcopal Church. They had friends who were Episcopalians. Teresa called Trinity on the Hill and made an appointment to talk to Fr. Kelly, who listened to her story with care and concern and assured her that she and her husband would indeed be able to receive communion the next Sunday. That was the Sunday when Teresa Gordon came home. "I realized then that I hadn't left the Roman Church—it had left me. Here in the Episcopal Church is the realization of all my hopes for Vatican II."

That doesn't mean the Episcopal Church has Teresa's complete and uncritical admiration in every detail. Home is also where you are entitled to express your views about the way the furniture is arranged and the quality of the evening meal. She thinks her rector has an unfortunate tendency to adopt an occasional "Romanish fad" like holding hands during the Lord's Prayer or using pottery chalices. But Teresa is now on the liturgy planning committee and head of the altar guild, so she lets her rector know when she feels that he has strayed too far from the dignified traditions to which she responds. She's not that happy with passing the Peace, either, and rather agrees with another parishioner who believes the Peace should be shared under NBA rules: "If you move both feet, that's 'traveling' and is not allowed!"

Of course, even the Episcopal Church does sometimes push Bible study at people and the Gordons have tried again. The rector tried to get a Bethel Bible study going one year, but they quit after four lessons, disgusted at the lack of intellectual depth. Jim is amazed they stuck it out that long but figures they wanted to give it an honest try. Even more amazing is the fact that Teresa then responded to an article in the paper about a new type of Bible study (the Little Rock Scripture Study series) for which a training course was being offered at IHM. Still resisting, still unconvinced that the Bible could hold anything of value for her and disturbed in particular by "that egomaniac John," Teresa went through the training course and became the moderator of a group of a dozen or so who worked their way through all the gospels as well as most of Paul, Isaiah, and the Psalms. Recently she felt led to read a book by Bishop Spong called *Rescuing the Bible from Fundamentalism.* She had heard mutterings about how he was an example of everything wrong with the Episcopal Church, but here, at last, was a way to look at the Bible that made sense to her. She wrote a review of it for the parish paper and sent a copy to the bishop to let him know that he had at least one admirer who is "a stodgy old normal housewife."

There is, Teresa knows well, a church beyond Trinity on the Hill. The Gordons have visited the cathedral in Salt Lake City and the parish church in Shawnee, Kansas, and the Episcopal Church looks to them like "a great and marvelous institution." Indeed, Teresa is sure that "for all practical purposes, the only place that could possibly be better than the Episcopal Church is heaven itself." And she prays: "I thank you, Lord, that by your grace you have led me into the Anglican communion of your holy church. Grant that I may continue in its fellowship all the days of my life, with your Son and Holy Spirit forever. Amen."

Colleen McMahon Sica will tell you that the story of her spiritual life is the story of a love affair, of how she was "seduced by God," a God who was willing to use whatever works, and who knew that what worked with Colleen was music.

Growing up in Columbus, Ohio, as the oldest of six children with deeply religious Irish Roman Catholic parents, Colleen McMahon was sent off to parochial school where worship, including music, was a part of every day. She loved it. The mass enraptured her. There were dull parts, of course, but you could always find something interesting to do. You might, for example, find a story like that of Susanna and the Elders in your *Daily Missal* that made for wonderful reading during the homily. And the music—the chants and the anthems—were as wonderful as television. When the nuns needed someone to play the organ for the daily mass, Colleen was the obvious choice. She was a musical child and also, by her own account, "a center-stage type of girl." Playing the organ gave her a chance to show off.

But it was the very same year that the nuns put Colleen at the organ that a worm appeared in her apple. New edicts came from Rome about the mass: no more Gregorian chant or Latin motets. Instead, it was folk music and pseudo-pop. Her fifth grade class was asked to write essays about how they liked the new mass and Colleen had nothing good to say. "This is awful," she thought. "Everything I love is gone."

Well, not quite everything. There was still the organ and Colleen got to play it every day all the way through grade school. When the time for high school came, Colleen went off to public school because the music program was better. And now there were opportunities to be literally on center stage: Colleen played the lead (Mary Martin's role) in *The Sound of Music*. She still played for the mass on some Sundays, and parlayed her skills at the piano and organ into a job as accompanist for the senior high school concert choir. Unlike her church, the public school had no new directives about the music they chose, so Colleen got to play some of the great religious music in the western tradition that was no longer in use at her church.

There's a certain strangeness about music: on the one hand, it is simply a matter of making vibrations with certain frequencies. Music has a correlation with mathematics, and those who are good at one often are good at the other. But music is not simply numbers and formulae; music also involves mystery. Music has a transforming power that opens up for many human beings a glimpse of the eternal. So it was with Colleen; God was using music as a door through which to enter ever more deeply into Colleen's life.

Toward the end of her eighth grade year, Colleen had a numinous experience. She had no way of knowing what it was at the time. The nuns did, of course, teach the children about the saints, and Colleen, a voracious reader, had devoured "thousands of books" about St. Thérèse of Lisieux and St. Catherine of Siena and St. Bernadette. But nowhere in all that reading had Colleen learned anything of the interior life of the saints. St. Thérèse, to her, was "a determined little girl who insisted on being admitted to a convent, was cheerful, brave, clean, and reverent, wrote a book called *The Little Way*, and died at twenty-four." Whatever references there may have been to the mystical life had passed right over her head. Colleen was a doer, an activist; kneeling in rapt adoration was not even "a blip on my radar screen." Certainly she had learned no words that could describe what happened to her. The experience was simply a sense of the presence of God, "a kind of glow, a rapture." It lasted for three days and Colleen spent as much of that time as she could in church, holding on to the experience.

God may plant seeds, but the growth can be a long time coming. And there can be long dry spells in which nothing at all seems to be happening. For Colleen the dry spell began in college and lasted for sixteen years. She was a legalist, as many parochial school children learn to be. She knew the rules: you must be at mass by the time the offertory begins or it doesn't count for your weekly obligation. In college there are many distractions, many competing voices. Colleen began coming later and later to mass and finally one Sunday she misjudged so badly that the priest was chanting the *Sursum Corda* when she arrived—"which meant I'd blown it!" She turned around and walked out, thereby committing what she had been taught was a mortal sin.

Somewhat to her surprise, she woke up the next morning anyway. And for her that was it for a long, long time. "There was nothing the church offered me that interested me: no solace, no transcendence. Going to mass had become a chore, something you did because you had to. So when I found out I didn't have to, I stopped."

These were the years of the Vietnam war and the rising tide of protest. In Ohio, the era is marked forever as the time when students were shot down by the National Guard at Kent State. But Colleen was not involved. "I was not rebellious. Good girls didn't do drugs or throw things and I had great respect for authority—and a concern for my reputation." Colleen finished college with flying colors and went on to law school at Harvard. Music was wonderful, but it wasn't a career; at least it wasn't a career for a practical young woman from Ohio who still had enormous respect for authority and knew the desirability of doing the expected thing.

So Colleen went east for, she will tell you, "the best three years of my life. Cambridge was a candy store. There's no better place to go to school. It's a cultural smorgasbord. You couldn't take advantage of one millionth of it." As for religion, it simply wasn't part of the picture. She went to an Easter Vigil once because people said the music was great. And it *was* great; it was a concert. But there was no other reason to go to church.

Law students normally use their second summer to work as an apprentice in a law firm, and the choices made then can shape a career. Colleen's best friend's brother told her he thought she was a "Paul Weiss kind of person," so she interviewed with the firm for a summer job, got it, and was invited back when she graduated. The firm of Paul Weiss, Rifkind, Wharton & Garrison is a New York firm with a strong liberal tradition. Founded over sixty years ago, at a time when Jewish and Gentile lawyers did not work together, it began as a partnership between a Jew and a Gentile. It was the first firm in New York to have an African American associate and the first to have a woman partner. Public service is part of the fabric of the firm and it has always placed a heavy emphasis on *pro bono* work and political activity. The firm has been closely linked to the NAACP Legal Defense Fund and involved in such issues as the fight against the death penalty and the teaching of "creation science."

The bread and butter of the firm, however, is corporate commercial litigation. Those who have learned about lawyers from Perry Mason and the O. J. Simpson trial need to understand that being brilliant in front of a jury is not what lawyers do; most of them sit in small offices poring over legal papers and negotiating on behalf of clients. In 1976 Paul Weiss was one of the few large firms that actually litigated cases, ranging from libel to securities fraud, and from insider trading to sexual harassment in the workplace. To present these cases in court, Paul Weiss wanted an outgoing, flamboyant type of person who liked to play to a jury. A bright and ambitious star of the high school and college stage would fit the job description to a T. Colleen was in her element: here was a chance to be an actress and be well paid besides.

Colleen met Frank Sica after three years as a single working woman. He had been her brother's business school roommate and was moving up in the investment field as fast as Colleen was moving up in law. Neither of them had been to church in a while, but families had expectations and Frank and Colleen had gotten where they were by doing traditional things well. So it was natural to check out St. Patrick's Cathedral as a site for their wedding. Why not have their wedding in the biggest Roman Catholic church in the city? They learned that if they would present a certificate from their neighborhood church and attend the required Pre-Cana Conference, the cathedral was available.

The Pre-Cana Conference is the Roman Catholic Church's response to the increasing instability of marriage and the rising tide of divorce. It is a commendable idea but not always successful: to expect one weekend, however well planned, to overcome twenty or thirty years of experience and the pressures of contemporary society is asking a great deal. Marriage is often an occasion that brings people back to church after some years away and the Pre-Cana Conference is an opportunity to reconnect couples to the church at a critical time in their lives. In this case, however, it was an opportunity that was missed.

Frank and Colleen opted for the seven-hour "intensive" conference rather than the more leisurely weekend. "Let's get it over with" was their attitude. Under the circumstances, a longer conference might only have prolonged the agony. The conference was designed for people very different from Colleen and Frank. Most of those present were in their late teens, and half the brides were visibly pregnant. Part of the day was spent explaining "natural" methods of contraception; at one point, Colleen got out her birth control pills and put them on the table in front of her.

Frank made her put them away. She did, however, as an honest and forthright person with a desire to be helpful, go home and write a scathing analysis of the day's faults and send it to the cathedral. There was no response.

The wedding rehearsal, like the Pre-Cana Conference and the wedding itself, did nothing to bridge the gulf between couple and church. It took place several weeks in advance and involved all the half-dozen couples who would be married at the cathedral on the designated day. The priest who conducted the wedding was assigned to the duty shortly before the service. He had not met the couples in advance, nor did he ever see them again.

It was the spring of 1981 and a new era was about to begin: a time of unlimited possibility for those who had the kinds of skills Colleen and Frank had. They saw themselves as "the ultimate Yuppie couple," and they were positioned to "have it all," whatever it might be. Professional couples can enjoy living in Manhattan until the first child arrives and begins to walk. Then, suddenly, they notice the lack of grass and play space and begin to wonder about schools. Their daughter Katie arrived in 1983, and soon was beginning to walk. Since Colleen and Frank held to the traditional vision of a house with a wide lawn on a winding street and children playing happily together, the time had come to look for the house with the sweeping lawn.

They decided to buy a home in an affluent suburb. Frank thought that meant Greenwich, Connecticut, but Colleen had visions of being a judge and that required her to stay in New York. Besides, Greenwich is almost an hour away and Colleen thought that was too long. It never occurred to either one to give up career for children, but it did occur to Colleen that the longer commute would mean less time at home. They decided to look in Westchester County, just north of the city, where several villages offer a good school system and a reasonable commute to midtown. They moved to Bronxville in 1985.

Frank and Colleen were also sure that their children needed a basic supply of "values." The obvious source was a church—not for them, of course, but for the children. And when the time comes to take the children to church, the traditional husband assumes that his wife will take care of that chore. So Colleen went off to find a church.

Katie had, in fact, already been baptized because Colleen had promised her mother on her death bed that she would see to that. And so, on a chilly day in December 1983, they had carried the infant to L'Eglise Notre Dame on Morningside Drive and a priest had poured water on her and said the necessary words. Colleen and Frank had found one friend who seemed suitable for the role of godparent, but not a second, so the priest had to help them out by coopting someone to stand in as the second witness.

So Katie was marked as a Christian, but where would her mother take her to learn what that might mean? St. Patrick's Cathedral was a fine setting for the wedding and Notre Dame was acceptable for a baptism, but for a continuing relationship it never occurred to Colleen to look for the nearest Roman Catholic Church; she had left that behind in Ohio. Being a Roman Catholic, she knew full well, meant playing by the church's rules and that she could not do. Colleen was ambivalent about abortion, but she was clear that she couldn't accept the Roman stand on birth control. Nor could she, as an emancipated, successful, late-twentieth-century woman, accept the second-class citizenship that seemed to be all Rome could offer to women. She loathed the post-Vatican II liturgy, which had taken away the music and the pageantry and the mystery, and she could not stomach becoming a "cafeteria Catholic": choose one practice from column A and two from column B and that will satisfy your conscience. "If I don't adhere to the rules," she realized, "I'm not one of them. The One True Church vaccine had worn off." The time had come to look for alternatives.

So where does one look for "values" when Rome is no longer an option? Colleen decided it would involve a search, trying first one church and then another, until something seemed to fit. And the place to begin was the Episcopal Church. Why? "Because I'm an Anglophile. I'm not Irish; I'm American. From fifth grade on, I enjoyed learning English history so I felt I knew something about the Episcopal Church. It's the English Church and I love England." She also knew a little bit about Protestant churches, having subbed as an organist here and there during high school years. She knew that for her "they were sterile. There was nothing there that spoke to me."

Christ Church, Bronxville, stands on a rising slope at the north end of the railroad station. It isn't hard to locate, but in those days it wasn't easy to get there at the right time. The parish was going through a time of experimentation; the sacred hour of eleven was no longer so popular as it had been. Thus a paid choir sang to a dwindling number of the elderly at 11 a.m. and the larger family congregation at an earlier hour was beginning to wonder about the church's use of its resources. So a ten o'clock compromise was being tested on the first Sunday of the month. The first three times she tried, Colleen arrived at the church at the wrong time and when she finally got it right, what she found was Morning Prayer at eleven o'clock, beautifully sung, to a handful of the faithful. It wasn't at all what she had known in Ohio, but nevertheless she knew at once it was home. When she finally found the family eucharist with its traditional liturgy and wonderful hymnody, there was no doubt at all that she was where she wanted Katie "to get some values."

But God's agenda extended beyond Colleen's. "I was being worked on," she realized later. "It began to be important for me to go every week. I wasn't analyzing it at the time, but something more was beginning to happen." At first it was the community that mattered to her. Christ Church was the first place in Bronxville where Colleen discovered a community. There was a progressive dinner and a chance to make new friends. Also, their family was growing: Patrick had followed Katie and, when Brian was born in 1989, there were three children who saw their parents only sleepily at daybreak and briefly at the end of the day. Colleen was not satisfied with that and, after five years as a partner in the firm, was in a position to take a year off.

Colleen now had more time to get involved at church and school, and she did. She went on field trips with her children's classes and joined with a few others to form a new group at the church. They called themselves CSF: Community, Service, Fellowship. They intended to work together to serve others and have some fun doing it. They took on the work of making sandwiches for "the Midnight Run," a local volunteer project to take food and blankets to homeless people in New York City. They made meals for a soup kitchen in Yonkers and developed a sister-parish relationship with a small church in an impoverished area of nearby Mount Vernon. They brought children from Mount Vernon to a children's pre-Christmas festival, the "Santa Saturday." Some of them attended services in Mount Vernon to get better acquainted with the community between Bronxville and the Bronx.

But music was the real lever. Colleen joined the choir, which regularly sang the finest church music, from the great polyphonic anthems of the English Reformation—"perfect for my forty-something boy soprano"—to the masterpieces of the twentieth-century English Church. She started playing the organ again, accompanying the choir during Holy Week, and began to take voice lessons for the first time. That was the year they "cemented me in serious concrete at Christ Church," Colleen recalls. But now she was also beginning to glimpse the God at work in her life. "God was using what worked, and what worked with me was music. Music was the hook. I was being prepared to become aware again of the presence of God."

In fact, the Spirit was working at more than just making Colleen aware of God's presence. There was work to be done, and Colleen would need that sense of presence in the tumultuous years ahead. In the spring of 1991, the parish was embarking on a long-term planning process. An archdeacon had been called in as a consultant and the vestry and parish leadership gathered for a full day of work. The day went well; some issues and potential solutions began to emerge. Then, just as the archdeacon was beginning to take down the newsprint and fold it up with a feeling of accomplishment, a man who had been quiet all day long spoke up. "We're spinning our wheels," he said, "and some of us want to get some action."

The archdeacon, who had been under severe physical stress due to an undiagnosed tumor, had gotten through the day with the help of some painkillers that were wearing off. This was not the time to be blindsided with a new agenda. He turned the remark aside and closed the session. Colleen, who hadn't met him before, walked to the front of the room. "What was that about?" he asked. "It's a long story," she answered. "I'll call you."

One telephone conversation led to more. The archdeacon was not the only one in crisis. Colleen was turning forty and had met failure for the first time in her life: she had just been turned down for the judgeship she very much wanted. Besides that, the perfect marriage was facing its midlife crisis, three growing children were making increasing demands, and the law firm was about to enter the "New Economic Era" of the nineties with a jolt. Colleen was on the vestry of a parish with wonderful liturgy and music, but also with people who had radically different visions of where they should be going. Life was full—more than full—and Colleen would need more than her abundant energy and intelligence to deal with it. The archdeacon sensed this and gently, very gently, prodded. He sent along some notes on the parish's planning process and tucked in a little book on contemplative prayer with a note: "I'd like to know how you react." Over the next year or so at least two dozen little books came her way from the archdiaconal office. She read them. She found herself staying after vestry meetings to spend some time in the church.

Now Colleen began to explore prayer in a new way. In the first place, there was intercessory prayer, something for which she feels "no natural gift." But clearly she was being called to pray for the archdeacon in his physical crisis and the parish in its turmoil. And then there came again a sense of God's presence and that numinous experience she had had as a child in Ohio, a sense of "wonderfulness, a feeling that 'God's in his heaven, all's right with the world.'" Prayer became an ongoing conversation: "Hi! Gorgeous day. Nice to feel you with me." When she felt the urge for a midday break with God, she walked five blocks to her "city parish"—the aforementioned Church of St. Mary the Virgin, which she describes as "the church of my childhood." Eventually, she would spend a year doing the Ignatian spiritual exercises as she tried to discern what God was calling her to do.

Over time, that call became louder and more insistent. With a deeper sense of God's presence came an urge to draw herself and the parish into a more active ministry to the community. The diocese was calling, too. She became the vice-chancellor, dealing with all types of diocesan legal problems. Sexual misconduct was emerging as a major concern and the bishop wanted someone with legal training to help chart a course through troubled waters. Hours of committee meetings produced a book one hundred pages long providing for the diocese clear guidelines and procedures based on open accountability and pastoral sensitivity. Retreats at nearby monasteries and a relationship with a seasoned spiritual advisor (a former Roman Catholic priest who was now an Episcopalian) helped provide the necessary anchor and time for reflection. And there was always the music—singing, playing, and even composing a setting for the mass.

Then, suddenly, in the middle of it all, the governor's office was on the phone. A judgeship was available; if she wanted it, she had fifteen days to wind up twenty years at the firm. Colleen was sworn in on a blistering day in the summer of 1995, ready to begin a new career that she sees as the ministry to which she has been called. Now more than ever, a sense of God's presence and a vision of the eternal city will be essential for survival.

This story is not finished. If God is, as Jesse Jackson likes to say, "not finished" with him, God has apparently just begun a new chapter—perhaps even a new volume—in the life of Colleen McMahon Sica. But a transition is always a good time for reflection. How does the Episcopal Church look to her at this juncture?

To Colleen, it looks like heaven. But it also looks like a church that does not take advantage of all its assets—and may, in fact, be in danger of fumbling them away. "For a variety of reasons," she says, "Anglicanism is out of step with the direction in which American spirituality is moving. The impetus today is for security achieved through rules, rules that don't change. That's what is fueling the movement away from the mainline churches and toward evangelical Protestantism. A gray, Anglican 'middle way' which eschews all but the non-negotiable, credal absolutes and emphasizes reasons rather than rules is not going to appeal to people who want that form of security. It can't appeal to them without fundamentally altering what it is."

However, she continues, laying out her case like a lawyer, "there are also people like me, who are leaving a church that is *authoritarian* and looking for one that is *authoritative*. That's the person for whom the mainline denominations are all 'competing.' It should come as no surprise that many of the people who fit that description—perhaps most—are disaffected Roman Catholics. With them the Episcopal Church should enjoy a tremendous advantage because, doctrinally and liturgically, it is remarkably similar to the sect in which they grew up. So it will feel familiar to them as it did to me. But first you have to get them in the door."

If it is indeed true that the Episcopal Church has a close affinity to the Roman Catholic Church in which many people grew up, what is it that appeals to those who have left Rome? "Well, I've talked to a number of people who fit that description," Colleen notes, "and they all tell me that the draw—or at least *a* draw—was the beautiful Anglican liturgy." There are many people, she believes, who are "looking for someplace that recreates the Holy of Holies, the 'otherness' of God, if only for an hour a week. The Episcopal Church reaches for the transcendent in worship. It employs the trappings of worship that have recreated the numinous throughout history—color, poetry, light, music, choreography, ritual. Episcopal parishes ought to play that card, ought to make themselves known for their liturgy. They ought to publicize the fact that here you can find liturgy that exalts God and appeals to the visceral sense of holiness deep inside each one of us. Frankly, I've never understood why our beautiful ceremonial and great music were such a well-kept secret."

"Anglican liturgy," Colleen concludes, "can serve another function—ironically, the same function that authoritarian rules fill in evangelical sects. It provides the immutable, the security blanket we all long for, the sense of God's eternal changelessness amid the turmoil of a changing world. That's kind of neat, when you think about it," says the lawyer, resting her case. As for herself, "I was carefully educated not to find security in the Episcopal Church." Nor has she; but she has found something that may be more important: a church in which the insecurity that goes with freedom is accepted and sometimes even valued since it provides room to change and grow in response to the call of love.

In both these stories, as in the stories of Hope Adams and Jerry Lamb, people who had grown up in the Roman Catholic Church felt that they were finding home by becoming Episcopalians. They had learned to value certain forms of music and liturgy and found something in the Episcopal Church which fit that value system. What they found, of course, was also different in many ways from what they had once known. Teresa Gordon and Colleen Sica had valued Gregorian plainsong and incense, but the Episcopal Church uses both only sparingly. They had grown up with celibate priests and polychromed statues. The churches they walked into had neither. In what sense was this new and different world truly "home"?

Ancient Greek philosophers puzzled about a similar problem. They wanted to understand how different objects could be recognized as related. How, for example, can we give the name "chair" to something upright, wooden, and brown, and to something low-slung, made of metal and red cloth, and even to something else of a roundish form, made of bright green plastic? The taste, touch, feel, and appearance of all these is radically different, yet we know immediately that each is a chair. The Greek philosophers decided that there must be an ideal chair somewhere, in heaven perhaps, of which all human chairs are more or less imperfect copies.

Is it possible, then, that when Roman Catholics speak of finding "home" in the Episcopal Church, they are not so much recognizing something they used to know as something they have never known, of which both churches are imperfect copies? Perhaps what they are saying is that their upbringing sensitized them to certain values which neither church expresses perfectly but which seem to them at this time to be better reflected in the Episcopal Church. When Hope Adams sat in the back of the church in Evanston checking the Episcopal prayer book against the Roman missal to see "whether they were doing it right," perhaps she should have been checking both books against some ideal pattern which no church fully possesses.

The Epistle to the Hebrews speaks of saints and martyrs who "confessed that they were strangers and pilgrims here" and who "looked for a city which has foundations, whose maker and builder is God." Jesus spoke of a "kingdom," which is both coming and already here. The Book of Revelation paints a glowing picture of a "new Jerusalem" coming down from heaven to take the place of the old, imperfect Jerusalem. Again and again, we are given pictures of the church as something in process, already here and yet not perfectly here. What we have now is only a foretaste of what will be. "Heaven is my home," says an old spiritual. The Catholic Church gives us a taste for that home and even the imperfect copies of it we find in New York and Kansas and Oregon can convey peace and joy and beauty.

But there is one more question to ask. Why, if both churches are Catholic and have almost identical liturgies, should the Episcopal Church convey that sense of home more deeply for some? Perhaps there are other factors that shape the way each church approaches liturgy and the value it places on it, factors that help explain why a young woman from Ohio who had grown up with a sense of rules and obligation and authority would find something freeing in the familiar liturgy and music of the Episcopal Church. It is important, then, to know that at the time of the Reformation in the sixteenth century, when the western church was torn apart by arguments about doctrine, the Church of England tried not to become involved. There were, of course, English Christians who agreed with Luther or Calvin or the pope, but rather than choose sides, the Church of England centered its attention on the Prayer Book and decided that it was more important to be united in worship than in doctrines and decrees. While Roman Catholics learned to look to the pope and papal pronouncements for unity, and Protestants learned to draw up statements of what they believed, Anglicans learned to look to the Prayer Book. Both churches had a liturgy, but Roman Catholics had something else and Anglicans didn't.

Worship, therefore, is truly the center of church life for Episcopalians and it is something we take part in not because we are required to, but because we have no other center—and that makes it "home" for us in a way it seldom is for other western Christians. We go to school and work because we have to, but they are not home. Home is where we go because it is the center of our lives and the place where we want to be. And when we are where we want to be, that is where love and joy and beauty are likeliest to be found.

3

Belonging

Steve Roman and Tony Merlo

"It makes me feel good about the Episcopal Church that there's no part of my background I have to throw away. My roots are recognized and honored." *(Steve Roman)*

"I need a liturgical service. I need that much structure. That's in my background and it's what I've found in the Episcopal Church. There's enough room and enough structure." *(Tony Merlo)*

You go to a church for the first time and there, hanging on a hook on the back of the pew ahead of you, is a little card that says: "Welcome. We hope you will let us know how we can be helpful." The card has a choice of items to be checked, ranging from "Please add my name to the parish list" to "Please pray for _____." Among the choices offered is usually one that says, "I would like someone to call on me." Now, on a first visit, this option may seem a bit threatening; after all, you may not be sure yet how you feel about this unfamiliar place and these unfamiliar people. But sometimes everything seems to fall into place: you feel at home in this church, you like the service, you've been searching for a place that felt right and this place does. So you check the line that says, "I'd like a visit." What will happen next?

The conventional wisdom is that newcomers should be called on within twenty-four hours, whether they turn in such a card or not. Strike while the iron is hot. Sometimes a committee of lay people is prepared to visit and respond to newcomers' questions. Often the pastor of the congregation will respond. But Tony and Kelly Merlo waited almost two weeks in the fall of 1992 before anything happened. Then, on a cold evening, when Tony was feeling a bit down with the flu and the Merlos would have been reluctant to have even their best friends in, the doorbell rang. There at the door was a committee of three from the church: the assistant pastor, another staff member, and a lay woman. "Hello," they said, "we're from St. Stephen's, and we're here because you checked one of those cards and said you'd like a visit."

What could they do? They asked for it and so here it is. Once inside, the committee of three introduced themselves and thanked the Merlos for coming to St. Stephen's, Sewickley, and asked how they could be helpful in answering any questions. Ellie Oliver, the lay woman, held the baby so Kelly and Tony would be freer to talk. And they did talk, in rather general terms, for quite a while. Before they left, the assistant pastor took out a little metal thing and unscrewed the top and anointed Tony with oil for healing, while Tony was thinking, "Wow, this is weird—this is too far out for me. This is my living room. What is this?" But, all the same, Tony and Kelly went back to St. Stephen's the next Sunday.

Two weeks later, it happened again. The Merlos were sitting at home one evening when the doorbell rang and there was this three-member committee again. They were no longer unfamiliar faces but, as Tony remembers it, "I was still thinking, what are you doing here?" This time, however, the committee members were much more focused. Now they were talking about doctrinal issues and eternal salvation. Now they were ready to pop the big question: "If you were to die tonight, are you sure you would go to heaven?"

Let's be clear about it: this is not what usually happens when people decide to join the Episcopal Church. St. Stephen's Church has its own approach, which includes a "thank you for visiting" letter within twenty-four hours and a visit of three lay people within two weeks. The Merlos' team included the assistant pastor because there was a new lay person being trained. And they don't make appointments because they find that it's too easy for people to tell them that whatever times are suggested are inconvenient—the Merlos surely would have told them that.

Although there isn't a single pattern Episcopal churches follow in responding to newcomers, there is a procedure that most parishes follow in one way or another. Once or twice a year they offer an inquirers' class or something similar. People who want to join the Episcopal Church attend these classes and then, when the bishop comes for the annual visit, they are confirmed, if they come from a Protestant background, or they are received, if they have already been confirmed in the Roman Catholic or Orthodox Church. Teresa Gordon, Colleen Sica, and Hope Adams all followed this pattern but, significantly, Teresa and Colleen never mentioned it in telling their stories and Hope mentioned it only in passing. It seems not to have been an important stage in the process for them. And perhaps it is significant to notice how the dramatic moment for each was that Sunday when they came to the communion rail for the first time and found themselves accepted and fed, with no questions asked. Tony and Kelly Merlo also had received communion more than once before the visitors from the church came to ask about their intentions. In a sense, they had already been welcomed into the family—and felt welcomed—before anyone came around to say so.

Membership in a family belongs to those who are welcome at the family table, and the Episcopal Church identifies members primarily by the criterion of baptism. Those who are baptized may come to the table. Those who are baptized, then, are already members of the family in the most important aspect of its life. The normal process of inquirers' class and the bishop's visit is less dramatic and significant than baptism, with none of the emotional and theological importance of coming to communion. Sometimes, as we will see, the question of membership is deliberately down-played and even ignored.

In our day at least, membership in the Episcopal Church seems to involve something more like a process of growth than a sudden change from darkness to light. There was a time—and still is in certain areas of the world—when becoming a member of the Christian church involved discarding the pagan idols or voodoo ceremonies and completely reorienting one's life. Even in the

United States today, the word "conversion" often seems to be limited to a radical change of life, a moment of dramatic change. But that is much too narrow an understanding. Conversion is, in fact, a life-long process which may or may not include dramatic moments but through which life is turned more and more completely toward a God who has been at work inwardly before we were ever aware of that fact.

So, for those whose stories we are telling in this book, the change from one church to another is simply one step in an ongoing journey. It began with the nurture they received in the Roman Catholic Church and continues after coming into the Episcopal Church. What happens involves a growing recognition that they are already Episcopalians in many ways, since that is the church where they are most completely at home, and what is needed is simply to recognize that fact and continue the growth to maturity.

Tony Merlo came to an Episcopal church that pushed for a decision. Steve Roman, on the other hand, came to a church that preferred to stand back and wait to see what direction his growth would take. But both of them, like Teresa Gordon and Colleen Sica, felt at home when they came into an Episcopal Church for the first time and perhaps that is what matters more than the very different ways in which they were welcomed. Here, then, are two stories that throw some light on what it means to "belong."

S teve Roman is an airline pilot and he likes to arrive on time. That's why it annoyed him one day a few years ago to find that he was late for mass. Steve had never liked the way so many people would come late for mass and leave early. But here he was at the door of the church, long after ten o'clock, and the mass that he thought began at ten-thirty had actually begun a half hour before. What to do?

As it happened, Steve had an alternative. Right across the street from Sacred Heart Church in Kent, Connecticut, is the parish hall of St. Andrew's Church, and the front door of St. Andrew's is just around the corner. The second eucharist of the day at St. Andrew's is at 10:30. What could be more convenient? So Steve went to church that Sunday at St. Andrew's. It was an experience he has never forgotten.

"I came out," he recalls, "feeling as if I were walking on air. I was excited about the people I had met who were friendly and welcoming, who introduced themselves and invited me back. And the homily was the best I had heard in years. The mass was very traditional, very familiar, and the music was older music, beautiful music, that people really sang." Steve has a theory that they remove the vocal chords at baptisms in the Roman Catholic Church and people never get them back, but these people had somehow survived baptism without losing the ability to sing. "I went back and called Chris, my fiancee, and said, 'You won't believe what I did. We've got to go together next week and check it out.'" So they did, and St. Andrew's has been a regular part of their lives ever since.

Having told this story, Steve is quick to add that his arrival at St. Andrew's wasn't really quite as impulsive as it sounds. Airline pilots don't change course on an impulse. Steve and Chris had agreed when they became engaged that they would not be a divided family; they would find one church that worked for both of them. Chris was an Episcopalian and they had visited her home church in Sherman, Connecticut, already and they had attended Roman Catholic masses in several different churches a number of times. But they had bought a house in Kent to live in after their marriage and St. Andrew's was on their list of churches to check at some point. On this particular Sunday, Chris was tied up and Steve had figured on simply going to Sacred Heart by himself and exploring St. Andrew's later. So the mistake in the time only expedited the discovery process.

That discovery process had, in fact, been going on for quite some time. Steve Roman grew up in a rather conservative Roman Catholic family. His mother, who grew up in the Baptist tradition, had become a Roman Catholic when she married. Nor was acceptance of her husband's church just a matter of convenience for Mrs. Roman. She studied her new faith and she liked what she found. So Steve and his two younger sisters were raised by faithful parents who wanted Steve to grow in the same faith that meant so much to them.

There was no parochial school in the little Connecticut town where they lived, but Steve went to CCD after school and served for years as an altar boy. When it came time for high school, his parents sent him to the Canterbury School in nearby New Milford, which, despite the Anglican sound of its name, is not at all related to the Episcopal Church. Canterbury is, in fact, an old New England preparatory school created specifically to give Roman Catholics the kind of college preparation that Episcopalians traditionally received at Kent and Groton School and a dozen other similar places.

Steve's parents were working to see that Steve would get the best possible education within the Roman Catholic tradition. And he did, but he also learned at Canterbury to look at his faith in new ways. Among the faculty members at the school was the Rev. Brendan McCormick, a former Benedictine monk who taught theology and who within a few years would join the Episcopal Church himself. So the teacher was also on a journey and, inevitably, his own pilgrimage was reflected in his teaching.

During the years when Steve Roman was at Canterbury, Fr. McCormick made it a priority to ask the students to look very seriously at the same questions he was asking himself about what is essential to the faith and what is peripheral. He wanted the students to approach their faith with an open mind, to think, to challenge, to grow. He taught the students to look at the Bible not as a static book of unchanging laws, but as a collection of books written at certain times in history and reflecting the particular concerns of the people by whom and for whom they were written. If Christians understood better the issues those people had faced, they would understand better the ways in which the Bible speaks to us today.

Suddenly, for Steve the Bible became a living book written by real people and speaking to real problems. Now, not every teenager will respond to the study of theology and the Bible, no matter how challenging the teacher, but Steve found it stimulating and exciting. It was his first experience of a more liberal way of looking at things; it helped him make sense of his faith and he liked that.

Fr. McCormick also wanted to communicate to his students some sense of the sacredness and dignity of human life and of its corporateness, as opposed to the individualism so often held up as central to American experience. He kept two symbols in his rooms: the cross and Noah's ark. The cross symbolized what he calls "radical incarnation," the deep involvement of God in this world through Jesus Christ and the church. The ark was a symbol of community, the life which all God's creatures share. These two symbols made him something more than a classroom teacher. He had established a program of social service at Canterbury to give students an opportunity to get involved in the lives of other people with special needs. There was a swimming program for mentally retarded children, a training program for retarded adults, and a program at a children's center. About a third of the students became involved in this program to some extent and half of those made it—in competition with the wide variety of sports programs and other activities offered at the school—a high priority. Steve Roman was one of the latter group. Helping others seemed to him a very logical way to express his faith.

Graduation from the small community and carefully regulated life at Canterbury to the large and open campus of the University of Connecticut was a traumatic change for Steve. Neither the village of New Fairfield nor the Canterbury School offered anything approaching the diversity and sheer numbers of the students at the university. Steve found the campus "overwhelming. I thought I'd better check out the church," he recalls. He knew he needed an anchor, and found it in the Roman Catholic chaplaincy program and a course called "Catholic Beliefs" taught by a Paulist priest who believed in questioning and growing, and who challenged the students to think and grow with him. This priest encouraged students to think about the role of conscience in decision-making, and how an informed conscience is each individual's final arbiter: Christians study the church's teaching, he taught his students, and they do their best to understand, but if, finally, they cannot choose what the church teaches, their conscience must be followed. Each semester there were retreats with an opportunity to explore issues of the Christian life in greater depth, to think and pray and know the presence of God in silence as well as community.

Other Christian traditions were active at the University of Connecticut as well. The Campus Crusade for Christ was there "bombarding you and telling you what you had to believe," Steve remembers. But that was the kind of narrow legalism that Steve was learning to question. All the other Paulist priests with whom Steve Roman came in contact created a warm and accepting environment at the college. No particular point was made about it, but no one was excluded, not even from receiving communion. Once there was an ecumenical liturgy—not a mass—shared with Episcopalians. Steve remembers sitting around and saying "Gee, you're not too different from us; let's see if we can find something we disagree on." They managed to come up with the church hierarchy and the Vatican as areas of disagreement, but that was all they could find.

His admiration for the Paulists developed into at least one lasting friendship and Steve wondered whether he himself might be called to join the order as a priest. He went to a formation retreat, but he felt the other potential candidates were not of the same caliber as the Paulists he knew; the idea of spending years of preparation with them was not appealing, nor was the idea of forsaking the possibility of marriage.

Steve went ahead with a major in communications and mass media with a focus on journalism, graduated, and found a job with a travel company located near Logan Airport in Boston. The job was boring beyond belief, but the windows of the office building overlooked the airport. Steve's father is a pilot and Steve remembered going for a ride with him occasionally when he was growing up. "There's something in the blood," he says. The constant sight of airplanes landing and taking off was an unbearable counterpoint to the immovable desk in front of him. He quit his job, took a one-year training course, completed it in nine months, and signed on with American Eagle, a commuter airline which soon had him running flights in and out of New York's JFK airport. So Steve came back home to northwestern Connecticut, commuting to the airport for his times of duty.

And then he met Chris. He was mowing the lawn one day when a neighbor came by and said, "Steve, there's a helicopter pilot I want you to meet. Come on, get in the car." Chris, it turned out, had also attended Canterbury School after Steve, went on to the University of Michigan, and then came back to Connecticut to begin a career teaching English as a second language—a specialty needed these days even in the small towns of rural northern Connecticut. But Chris felt her life needed a change of pace, and now she was expanding her horizons by learning to fly a helicopter. A leisurely flight down along the winding shoreline of Lake Waramaug and back over the familiar rooftops of their Sherman and New Fairfield hometowns led them to believe that they had a good deal in common and should meet again. The wedding took place in the chapel of Canterbury School.

But first Chris and Steve set out to find a church where both would be comfortable, and they began by introducing each other to the churches where they had grown up. Steve liked Chris's home parish in Sherman well enough, and the priest assured him that he was welcome to receive communion—but it was Chris's church, not Steve's, and it was not where they were going to live.

As for the several Roman Catholic churches they explored together, they discovered two recurring themes: abortion and the budget. Seven times they went to mass together and always it included a sermon on abortion or the budget. Chris looked at Steve one day and said, "I feel so bad for you, because I know you want me to like this." And Steve said, "Chris, I don't like it either." They went to several more masses and when the homily came and the same themes were broached, they would nudge each other and roll their eyes. Surely there were other things to talk about. Canterbury and the University of Connecticut had offered so much to Steve; the Paulists had talked often about social issues, how we have a responsibility to the person next to us, especially those in need. It was hard to believe they couldn't find something of that same openness and challenge at the parish level. They kept looking, but it didn't seem to be there. And then Steve discovered St. Andrew's, and knew he was home.

Roger White, the rector, greeted Steve at the door. "Can you stay and have a cup of coffee?" Steve walked back to the parish hall and Roger was quick to introduce him to others. "I'd like you to meet Tod Jones, and Craig, and Bill." It was a new experience of parish life for Steve. There was no coffee hour where he grew up; people were on their way out before the mass was really over. But community is a big issue for Steve; it was an important part of what made his university years so special. It made St. Andrew's special, too.

It wasn't long before Steve and some of the other men he met that first morning had formed a discussion group to get together after church on Sundays and discuss the readings. They are a diverse group, each with his own particular slant on the Bible and, though the rector sometimes joins them, they learn mostly from each other. Craig has a good grasp of theology and a common sense approach. He has a way of putting things in perspective, of tying it all together. Tod loves the imagery of Revelation, a book that Steve is "not real comfortable with" because it seems to present a remote and forbidding view of God sitting on a throne and looking down. Steve wants practical answers to practical questions: "What does this do for us here and now? How can I get some practical guidance out of this?" The Trinity makes sense to Steve because it includes us and connects us with God.

And so did St. Andrew's Church. Steve already knew that he was welcome at communion because Chris's rector in Sherman had told him. But Roger White puts a notice in the Sunday bulletin each week: "All baptized Christians are invited to make their Communions at St. Andrew's Church this morning." That invitation to communion matters in a larger way to Steve. He's aware of the tensions in the Episcopal Church over sexual issues and thinks there should be no prejudice against people who are homosexual. Should an openly gay individual be ordained—be rector, perhaps, of Steve's parish? Steve has no difficulty with the idea but knows that others might. "I could accept it," he says, "but I wonder if, in a small, conservative parish, such a person might have trouble being a leader. That's why it's so good that the Episcopal Church lets each parish choose its own leadership. Each individual has gifts and talents and the church has a place for them. I'd like to see the church be as accepting and loving of all kinds of people as it can be."

There are those who come to a town like Kent to escape the problems of the outside world, but others who feel a need to be involved and do what they can with the gifts they have been given. Roger White supports such people and makes it clear in his preaching that the gospel has social consequences. The same themes Steve responded to at Canterbury and the University of Connecticut are standard fare in the pulpit at St. Andrew's and preaching is expressed in action.

There is, for example, an AIDS support group in Kent organized first by parish members at St. Andrew's and then deliberately broadened to include the larger community. Vigils have been held in front of St. Andrew's and the names of those who have died are read. A forum was held to raise awareness and that, in turn, led parents to go to the principal of the local grade school and ask for a fuller program of AIDS education for their children. This is a parish that helps a community change to meet new challenges.

"Ideally," Steve will tell you, "I'd like a job giving more to people's needs. Right now what I do is volunteer. I started doing that when I was in school and now I'm getting back into that as an important part of my life." Steve's particular form of service to others flows naturally from his skill in carpentry, a skill acquired through six summers and part of several winters as he worked to help put himself through college. Carpentry had been useful again as Chris and Steve set out to renovate the old house they bought on a quiet side street in Kent. The kitchen is the room Steve brings visitors to, partly because it's a bright, pleasant place to sit, and partly because he built it himself and takes a certain pride in showing it off. He volunteers with a local chapter of Habitat for Humanity, which he sees as "a way to give back a little bit of what I've been given." There are committee meetings on Wednesday nights and Steve is a member of the building committee. Most recently, the group has been working on a couple of two-family units in New Milford. The site required blasting and major excavating equipment, but somehow they found people to provide what was needed. On Saturdays when he's not flying, Steve is there with saw and hammer to make a difference with his own hands.

Now, you might expect the story to end here with a report on how Steve was received into the Episcopal Church and is planning to live happily ever after, right? Wrong. This is, after all, the Episcopal Church we are talking about, and in this church one learns to live with ambiguity. A year or two after Steve started attending St. Andrew's someone asked him at coffee hour whether he was going to be received into the Episcopal Church. He answered, "What's 'received'?" It wasn't something Steve had heard about. And now that he has, he still doesn't give being officially received into the Episcopal Church much thought. "I felt like I was part of the community so completely, it didn't seem important."

And here we come to one of the central questions that is posed by these stories of Roman Catholics finding the Episcopal Church: what do we mean today by "church"? Is it a clearly defined body of people who have affirmed a common set of beliefs and agreed to abide by certain standards of behavior and practice, or is it something less clear, more subjective? Is it, we might ask, the institution that decides who belongs, or is it the individual who decides where he or she feels comfortable? Steve has experienced two radically different ways of defining church: "In the Roman Catholic Church you have to be confirmed and have first communion, but the Paulists turned no one away. So all through college I had a very open experience. Communion, it seems to me, is for all people and artificial barriers only alienate people. We talked about it a lot at UConn. We asked 'What is this? Why are we excluding people if they are part of the body of Christ?'" The question for Steve is simple: "Do we take baptism seriously?" The statement in the bulletin at St. Andrew's makes it clear that this is one church that does: "All baptized people are welcome."

But being truly welcome, as his rector Roger White sees it, does not involve being captured: "My principal concern with Steve is not to make him feel as if we have somehow 'won' him.

It's not my job to lure people away from the Roman Catholic Church; it's an ancient and honorable faith. It seems to me that my obligation is to be clear about what we in this parish believe and do, and to encourage forgiveness for whatever wrongs others believe they've experienced. I don't know that Steve will always be an Episcopalian. He's not angry with the Roman Catholic Church. I'd be really and truly reluctant to push him toward being received unless he gave me a high sign that he's come to a new understanding of who he is. For most people it's a delicate growth that's happening, and to respond institutionally instead of personally is something to wonder about."

There is talk these days of a distinction that needs to be made between "first culture" and "second culture" Roman Catholics. Eugene Kennedy of Loyola University in Chicago thinks the church is dividing into two cultures, each with its own understanding of what being a church member involves. Those of the first culture are people who accept the institution on its own terms: a hierarchical church with clear rules of conduct that ought to be observed. Those of the second culture are, as the title of one of Kennedy's books describes them, *Tomorrow's Catholics in Yesterday's Church*. For them the traditional discussion of liturgical colors and the details of the Friday fast are simply irrelevant. There is much in the church's faith that they value, but it is they, not the parish priest or even the pope, who will decide how to live out that faith today.

Is St. Andrew's, by chance, a "second culture" parish? Roger White laughs at the idea. "No, I'm an old-fashioned Anglican. The town is my parish. If you live in Kent and come to St. Andrew's, you're a member." He stresses the value of a self-conscious living out of the baptismal covenant and the reaffirmation of baptismal vows, as opposed to confirmation and reception. With the former, the emphasis can be placed on growth in faith; with the latter, the stress seems to fall on something like a test act.

Inquirers' classes are held regularly at St. Andrew's and a high percentage of those attending choose not to be confirmed or received. "These are very private people," Roger will tell you, "and they come to deepen their understanding of what we do here. The idea of a public profession doesn't appeal, doesn't seem to them to have anything to do with the maturity of their faith. People today will tell you, 'I'm going to the Episcopal Church,' not 'I belong to the Episcopal Church.' It's not a brand of Christianity that people identify with, but a local parish church. For Steve, of course, it can't be just any parish; it has to be one that speaks a language he understands. The articulation of the faith needs to be recognizable: more than just words, it has to be also in terms of liturgy and ritual action."

But that means, of course, that second culture Catholics may be able to find in St. Andrew's Church a place where their language is spoken. Roger White does make a distinction, but the terms are very different: "There are people who want challenge and there are people who want reassurance. Steve is looking for challenge."

Steve will tell you that himself. "'Come, fill me up': that's our society in general, and I find it in the Episcopal Church, too." But on balance what he finds in the Episcopal Church is a healthier community, a church which, like Tony Merlo's church, is drawing people into ministry—although in a very different style. Steve thinks that the Episcopal Church is drawing "better" people into ordained ministry than is the Roman Catholic Church, but what may be more important is that the Episcopal Church is drawing people into lay ministry. For Steve, that is what counts. "I don't leave the Roman Catholic Church with any sense of anger," he adds. "I have problems with certain issues and the quality of the leadership. It makes me sad because I have had a good experience and I hope it will continue to give that experience to other people. It makes me feel good about the Episcopal Church that there's no part of my background I have to throw away. My roots are recognized and honored."

What matters to Steve is the way what happens on Sunday helps him through the week: "My faith helps me deal better with the people I come in contact with, to see the moral way to deal with the ground crew and passengers. If they aren't acting friendly, I take a deep breath and remember what Roger talked about at mass last week, and the discussion group helps a lot, too."

So this is not a story that comes to a clear and tidy conclusion; instead, it is the story of a life in progress, the story of someone who is looking for a church that can live with people in that process. It is the story also of a parish church that is open, welcoming, challenging, questioning, and more interested in helping people like Steve in their search for answers than in providing clear definitions and counting up those who salute.

Not every Episcopal Church takes the same approach to welcoming newcomers that St. Andrew's does. Conversion may be a lifelong process, but some churches like to challenge newcomers to make decisions. They think it is important to ask, "If you died tonight, are you sure you would go to heaven?" The visitors in Tony Merlo's living room asked that question and Tony had to admit he wasn't sure. "Right," said the assistant pastor. "We need to talk." So they studied the Bible and prayed awhile and the committee left. Somehow it felt all right to the Merlos. They still weren't ready to "do anything drastic" but they wanted to hear more, to explore the Episcopal Church seriously, to see whether this really was the church they had been looking for.

Even now Tony talks about his experience in finding a church as if it were part of a search process he had initiated rather than a conversion process in which God had taken the initiative early on, but he is convinced that God has been at work in his life from a very early age. If Tony is comfortable with visiting committees that ask ultimate questions, it may be because God had been acting dramatically in Tony's life for a long time and literally called him back from death for the first time at the tender age of three.

The Merlo family had been out Christmas shopping and they were coming home in the car. Tony was in the back seat and beginning to show signs of a fever. He got very hot indeed and suddenly threw up and went into convulsions. The Merlos headed the car toward the nearest hospital and Tony was taken into the emergency room, where the medical staff tried to do what they could. The mysterious seizures had by now escalated out of control and a shaken doctor came out to report to the parents that he was very sorry, they had done everything they could, but the child was dead. Mrs. Merlo collapsed in grief in the corridor and Mr. Merlo went into the room, devoid now of staff, and stood by the bedside praying. Anthony Merlo wasn't a praying man but this was a time when he had no real alternative to prayer, and so he prayed long and hard. He didn't know much about God, but he did know how to deal with people in power and he offered God a bargain: "Give me back my son, and I'll go to church every day." Suddenly he realized that the child was breathing. He rushed off to look for a doctor. "He's breathing! Come on, do something!" And so Tony came back to life.

Now, a story like that gets told and retold and Tony, growing up, heard it more than once. Uncles and aunts would nod and say, "God has a purpose for that boy." And Tony took it all with a grain of salt. How can a normal, healthy child take stories like that seriously? But when he was twelve he was back in the hospital for some minor surgery, adenoids perhaps, and a veteran nurse came into the room and said, "Are you really Tony Merlo? I remember the day you died." So then he knew for sure that it wasn't just something his parents made up. He also remembers how his father kept his end of the bargain and went to church every day as promised. Not to mass—that wasn't in the bargain—but most often, after dinner, he would walk down the street to the church and make a visit. "And when I get back from my visit," he would call out to his children as he went out the door, "I want you to have the dishes done."

So Tony and his siblings would do the dishes while their father paid his daily installment on his son's life. Whatever strange events may have happened in the past, life still goes on and the normal twelve-year-old has more pressing concerns than God's purpose for him. Nor was the Merlo pattern of family life one that centered very much on matters of faith and ultimate meaning. Anthony Merlo was a first-generation American whose parents had come to this country from Naples. He was a fireman in the Pittsburgh fire department and his life was focused on his work and his family; church was a secondary concern.

Of course the children were baptized, and until third or fourth grade, when money became too tight, the Merlos sent Tony to the parochial school. "I was tired of the nuns at that point anyway," he recalls, "and ready to be free." But still there was CCD and first communion: week by week, the senior Merlos got their children out of bed on Sunday morning and sent them off to the church—and then relaxed peacefully until the children got home again. They did go to mass at Christmas and Easter and special times, but Mr. Merlo would often talk about the hypocrisy of the priests and let it be known that his view of the church was more than slightly jaundiced.

The church of Tony's childhood memories was "a dark and scary place where I always felt fear. It was almost like a haunted house, a sense of spirits, the tabernacle looming. I never felt I could have a relationship with God except to fear and obey. I never felt any joy there." Tony's younger brother felt differently about it and wanted to be an altar boy, but was turned down because the family was behind on tuition payments for the parochial school. An irate Anthony Merlo yanked his son out of the parochial school and sent him off to the public school as well. But Tony never wanted to be an altar boy in the first place.

In his teens, however, Tony did receive one insight into another way of knowing God. Someone asked him if he would be willing to play his guitar for a Lutheran vacation Bible school, and this became his first real contact with another kind of Christianity. He asked one of the counselors in the program to explain the difference between Lutheranism and Roman Catholicism, and the counselor gave it to him in a nutshell: "You fear the Lord, but we love the Lord." Tony stored this new idea away to ponder on his own. He also remembers a dream from that period in his life, a vivid dream in which he saw the heavens opening up and the Lord descending while a choir sang "God so loved the world." That happened to be a song they had sung at the vacation Bible school, so Tony knew where it came from and didn't have to take it too seriously.

College wasn't part of the usual experience of first-generation Americans, and none of Tony's four older sisters had gone. But Tony, the first son, had visions of getting into broadcasting and went off to Penn State to take courses that would prepare him for a career in the communications industry. One of his friends suddenly "got religion" and began going to church. He invited Tony to go with him so he could "find the Lord, too," but what Tony found was a charismatic, fundamentalist church where people prayed and testified and spoke in tongues and "scared me to death." He ran out as fast as he could. But there was something all the same that seemed to keep intruding.

Quitting college after two years in order to "find something real to do," Tony found there wasn't much need for broadcasters but that the banks were looking for people with communications skills. He got a job with the Mellon Bank and began to work his way up the corporate ladder in the area of mortgage banking. More important, he met Kelly Ann Latimer and they were soon engaged to be married. Both of them Roman Catholics, there would be a nuptial mass in the church and required attendance at a Pre-Cana Conference. As Tony remembers it, the conference was led mostly by nuns and priests who talked about healthy sexual relationships. However much they may have known, since they couldn't speak much from experience the thirty or forty couples in the auditorium poked each other in the ribs and rolled their eyes. But there was a husband and wife team as well, and Tony remembers they talked about "burlap bagging": the habit of hanging onto a hurt or imagined wrong for months and then dragging it out of the bag and saying, "You did that to me!" For years afterwards, Kelly and Tony would use that phrase when it seemed that the other was using the burlap bag—and it did help to break the tension.

More significant, perhaps, to the work God was doing in Tony's life was an incident just before the wedding. His brother was diagnosed suddenly with a lymph node cancer for which no cure seemed possible. His parents were anguished and Tony remembers how members of the family would "sit around crying." Tony, upstairs, knelt in prayer—and received an answer: "Your brother will be healed." He tried to pass the good news on to his parents but didn't quite know how to tell them. If he said, "God told me," he knew they would think he had gone crazy. So he simply told them he knew his brother would get better and the family passed his news off as wishful thinking—but his brother did recover.

Perhaps it was this incident that led Tony to feel he had to take God's role in his life more seriously. Church wasn't a high priority for the newly married couple but Tony found a very small New Testament that included the Psalter and carried it to work with him in his pocket. He would read it when he had a few moments to himself, mostly in the company bathroom! Three years after the wedding, when their first child was born, Kelly decided it was time they went to church in order to set an example for the children. Tony took his Bible along and read it during mass. It annoyed Kelly and they argued about it, but Tony felt it was about the only way to get some benefit from the time he spent in church; he was determined not to recite "those empty prayers." As for talking to the priest about this strange feeling he had that God was trying to communicate with him, he just knew that wouldn't work. The priest, he figured, would tell him to say three Hail Marys and forget about it.

His furtive Bible reading continued, however, and it did make a difference. Tony came to understand that it is possible to communicate with a God you have never known—even in the Mellon Bank. Over time, it began to make a difference in his conduct, as passages like the Beatitudes started to shape his behavior. He kept two bookmarks in the Bible, one in the Old Testament and one in the New, and just kept reading consecutively. There were parts of the Old Testament that he skipped over pretty quickly, but he loved the history bits. He kept reading, and making his own interpretations.

Meanwhile, the bank had moved the family to Philadelphia, and the children were growing and going off to parochial school. Tony and Kelly played the part of good parents: Kelly got on committees and planned fundraisers while Tony and the other fathers came around when it was time to move tables and chairs and do the heavy lifting. It didn't provide much spiritual nourishment, but they did make some good and lasting friendships.

Monetary rewards began to flow in. Whatever toys they wanted, they could have. Tony even took flying lessons. "Worldly-wise," he reports of those days, "we were extremely happy." And they went to church on Sunday and Tony read his Bible during the mass and at other times when no one was looking.

Occasionally, however, he would look at the deacon and priest at the altar and feel some sort of urge. He even talked to the parish deacon about the diaconal program. But the program required a commitment of time and the financial rewards with the bank were too great for Tony to make that commitment, so he let it go. He was vice-president now for the Pennsylvania region and handling $120 million a year. It was going to take some major disruption to turn his attention from all of that.

Then Kelly went to Pittsburgh to visit her family and friends. From there she called Tony and said, "I want to move back to Pittsburgh." "No way," replied Tony. "It's a dead town. I'll never move back." He couldn't imagine what had gotten into Kelly and he went off by himself to a Phillies game to forget about it. It didn't work. He flew out to Pittsburgh to drive back to Philadelphia with Kelly and found himself saying, "Okay, I'll move." He found another bank that had a place for someone with his skills in the Pittsburgh office and the move was made. On Sunday they went to St. Joseph's Church and Tony went out of his way to shake hands with the priest: "I'm new in the neighborhood," he said, introducing himself, "and we'll be joining your church." The priest accepted the information but it didn't seem to matter. Tony got the feeling that one family more or less was not that important.

A different kind of welcome came from a neighbor. Barbara Filler, a woman Kelly had met in the neighborhood, asked her if she would like to join some other women for Bible study. They met Tuesday mornings at St. Stephen's Church, Sewickley, in the auditorium, thirty or forty women sitting in rows while a member of the staff gave a lecture. But there was time for social contact, too, and Kelly liked the group. More time went by, and one day she said to Tony, "I want to go to St. Stephen's some Sunday." "Okay," he agreed. "It's got to be better than what we're doing."

St. Stephen's was a good-sized church, with two or three hundred people at each of its three services. The Merlos "slid in and slid out" the way they had always done at St. Joseph's; they didn't talk to anyone and no one talked to them. But when they got back in the car and looked at each other, they said, "Wow!" Tony, impulsive as always, wanted to join: "I was floored by the energy I felt," he remembers. "The liturgy was familiar enough to be comfortable for me and as a musician, I just thought the music was incredible." They drove home talking about it and behind them at the church the visitor's card they had checked was duly noted.

It may have taken almost two weeks for St. Stephen's to respond to the card, but once they did, a system was in place. In February the Merlos joined a new members class that met every Wednesday night for twelve weeks. Some eighty other adults came together with no commitment to join, but a desire to know more about the Episcopal Church, its history and prayer book. Each Wednesday after a forty-minute lecture they met in small groups to talk about the lecture and to pray. Halfway through the course, Tony and Kelly knew they wanted to join the church: "We were two parched, dry souls, and they poured the Anglican faith all over us and it felt so good."

When the bishop visited St. Stephen's that spring, the Merlos were in a group of one hundred twenty people, two-thirds of them adults, who were presented to the bishop to be confirmed or received into the Episcopal Church. Not satisfied with all of that, Tony also signed up for a short course on the Old Testament, involving twelve weeks of home study and then a week at the nearby Episcopal seminary. At last he could get some guidance, some context, for all that Bible reading he had done over the years.

At St. Stephen's they don't confirm people and then leave them alone. Membership is being involved, not just showing up for an hour or so on Sunday. In June the Merlos were invited to join a group for weekly Bible study, and soon Tony was helping with the music and being invited to the next new members class to give testimony. Staff members also began meeting with Tony: sometimes twice a month, sometimes weekly over breakfast, someone would sit down with Tony and work with him. They had an idea that he ought to be leading a Bible study group and wanted to give him the training to do it. He already knew how to facilitate a group from his business experience, but now he was being introduced to prayer journaling and guided in his spiritual growth. He learned "how to dig into a Bible verse and pull out the meaning." The next winter, the home group split into three and Tony was responsible for leading one of them. Now he was a lay pastor and leading others in their journey.

Was it the fast-paced change in his spiritual life that made Tony sharply aware of his discontent with his career, or was it the increasing lack of comfort in his career that led him to put so much energy into spiritual growth? Whatever the relationship between the two may have been, it was at about this time that Tony realized he didn't enjoy his work anymore. The mortgage banking business was changing; increasing competition had led to a bidding war on rates and new underwriting guidelines. Tony had enjoyed the human aspects of the business, the building of relationships with clients and staff, but now it seemed that the whole emphasis was on paper and procedures. He had to drag himself to work in the morning and he knew he couldn't really motivate his staff if he wasn't motivated himself. Something had to change. He talked to some friends, raised some money, and set out to build his own business. But the timing was bad; in less than a year, the money was gone and he had to give it up.

The summer of 1994 was the worst in his life, and it put stress on their marriage to a degree that he and Kelly had never known before. He had a new and wonderful relationship with his Lord, but suddenly his Lord seemed to feel that he needed to learn something more about human limits, about trust, about depending on grace. Tony and Kelly forced themselves to stay together and keep talking as the rollercoaster of emotions rose and fell. By grace they survived and learned something more about the meaning of faithfulness.

A few months after his private venture failed, a friend made a contact for Tony that led to a new position in the title insurance business. He didn't have much background for the technical side of the work, but the staff knew that aspect of things and Tony could concentrate on what he was good at: motivating the staff and developing new relationships for the firm. "I love meeting people, converting them into clients, the challenge of getting people to say 'Yes,' the freedom to set my own goals." He and Kelly had talked about what they needed to look for in terms of income and they had two figures: a bottom-line survival number, and a higher number that would let them keep the kids in private schools. Tony asked for the lower number and was offered the higher, to the dollar. He figured someone was looking out for him.

Change begets change. Shake up one aspect of your life and you begin to look at the others. Now you have a new job and a new faith and things are going well. Yes, but suppose God wants even more? There had been those little urges all along the way; maybe it was time to explore them. Tony discussed the matter with the assistant pastor at St. Stephen's and then arranged to meet with the bishop and talk about his feeling of a vocation to the priesthood.

"Well," said the bishop, "the problem is that I don't really know you, and we already have more candidates than we have positions for. We're not accepting any more applicants. About the only thing I can suggest is that you do something really spectacular so we can't turn you down. Why don't you start a new church?"

"No," said Tony, "I don't think I'm ready for that. I don't know enough, for one thing, and for another, I would probably be drawing people away from the church where I am and I don't want to do that." But then he had an idea. St. Stephen's had just set up an arrangement to support a nearby church that had been struggling to survive. A new priest had been called and they hoped to turn things around, breathe new life into the place. "Why don't I go help at St. Phillip's," suggested Tony, "and that way I can get some experience and we can see what the next step ought to be."

And then he talked to Kelly about it: if he was thinking about being ordained, he realized, his wife probably ought to know! He should have told her sooner but he wasn't really sure how she would react to this idea of getting ordained, with all the changes that it would mean for their life. To Tony's surprise, Kelly had already thought of ordination: "I've seen it in you all along," she told him, "and I've been praying about it."

So that is where Tony is at the moment: enjoying his new job, giving as much time as possible to St. Phillip's, signed up to start taking a course at Trinity Episcopal School for Ministry, and waiting for guidance as to the shape his ministry should take. For now, it is a lay ministry—and very active. He and Kelly lead a course called "Home Builders" using the nondenominational program "Family Life Ministries," a program designed for couples and centered on the Bible. Tony also shares responsibility with his rector to keep six home Bible study and prayer groups going and they hope to have another six in place by the end of the year. Of course he's involved in the music, trying to give it a more contemporary feel to hold the younger couples. "We want to keep the back door shut!" he says. "Get the front door wide open and not let them get back out." He's also working on a program for men: "The church is too feminine—there isn't any place men can go to be spiritually fed." But Tony knows that problem from his own experience and he figures he can do something about it.

Has he found the right church? One Sunday recently he decided to do a reality check and talked Kelly into going to a nearby nondenominational church that seemed to be booming. He hated it. "The people were really friendly and they invited us back, but I couldn't wait to get out of there. The service was too free. They had prayers and then communion and then a sermon and then the offering. It didn't make sense. I need a liturgical service. I need that structure. That's in my background and it's what I've found in the Episcopal Church. There's enough room and enough structure. God is not a cosmic pushover, but I can have a relationship with him."

Enough room and enough structure. It's a difficult balance to maintain but it's a good definition of the church Tony Merlo has found.

We have suggested already that the word "conversion" is often used too narrowly to refer to one dramatic moment in life, but that, in fact, conversion is a lifelong process of turning and growing. As we hear stories about the ways people have become members of the Episcopal Church it begins to seem that the words "member" and "membership" are used too broadly. Americans today may have "membership" in organizations as various as the Masons or Michigan Militia, the Smithsonian Institute or the Sierra Club, a neighborhood bridge club or the Naval Reserve.

These various memberships also may bring very different changes to the lifestyles of different people. For a member of the Democratic or Republican Party, membership may involve trudging to the polls every year or two to vote in a primary election or it can mean numerous meetings year round and days and nights of frenzied activity in election seasons. In a similar way, membership in the Episcopal Church can mean a life centered at the altar and dramatically transformed in almost every way, or it may mean showing up in church at Christmas and Easter. Does the word "membership" serve a useful function if it includes so wide a range of meanings?

Serious questions are also being asked about what membership means to people in contemporary America. The individualism in which Americans have always taken great pride seems to be expanding dangerously. When Americans first moved out onto new frontiers, they found themselves free of the old world's weight of tradition but still required to work together with their neighbors to survive. Now, for many, survival seems to require not coming together but increasing separation in gated communities and heavily locked apartments. The television and video tape recorder in the living room or bedroom provide the entertainment that once was found in parish halls and community centers. Individualism is being transformed into isolation. And with this new and exaggerated individualism, whatever memberships we have can be seen as conveniences rather than necessities.

One observer of modern trends, Albert Borgman, tells us that:

> The heirs of rugged individualism take it for granted that they are free to marry or not, to have children whether they are or are not married, and to go their separate ways if they no longer want to be together. If they are of Norwegian descent but have a taste for Italian culture, they can turn to pizza, Pavarotti, and La Strada. If they dislike their Protestant upbringing, they may move to Catholicism or Buddhism. [1]

That freedom from the limitations of ethnic neighborhoods and identity, as noted already, frees us also to change churches more easily. Is church membership, then, simply one more optional extra in our lives, to change or drop as our moods shift and interests change? If it seems so, it may be because the Christian church has allowed membership to be defined in terms of particular denominations. Thus we consider ourselves to be "members" of the Episcopal Church, Presbyterian Church, or Roman Catholic Church and feel free to change our membership from one church to another while forgetting that we are also, more fundamentally, members of the body of Christ.

Both the Episcopal Church and Roman Catholic Church, however, define membership in terms of baptism. The Catechism in the *Book of Common Prayer* describes the church as "the Body of which Jesus Christ is the Head and all baptized people are the members." The *Code of Canon Law* of the Roman Catholic Church says that "the Christian faithful are those who...have been incorporated in Christ through baptism." [2] Baptism, in turn, is defined as a new birth into life in Christ. Thus, baptized membership in the church is a matter of identity, more like ethnicity than belonging to a club, since it is something that changes who the baptized person is and cannot be undone. The Roman Catholic *Code of Canon Law* goes so far as to indicate that every baptized person is a member of the (Roman) Catholic Church, though a commentary tells us that they are "joined in a certain, even if not perfect, communion with the Catholic Church." [3]

In this fundamental sense, the individuals who move from the Roman Catholic Church to the Episcopal Church do not change their membership, their essential identity as Catholic Christians. Indeed, they may speak of finding "home" because what they have found is a place in which to discover more fully and completely what that essential identity can be.

Notes

1. Albert Borgman, *Crossing the Postmodern Divide* (Chicago: University of Chicago Press, 1992), p. 39.
2. Canon 204 in *The Code of Canon Law* (Washington, D. C.: Canon Law Society of America, 1983), p. 69. The Presbyterian Church, on the other hand, defines membership in terms of faith in Jesus Christ and calls baptism "a visible sign of entrance into the active membership of the Church" (*Book of Order*, G-5.0101).
3. James H. Provost, *Code, Community, Ministry: Selected Studies for the Parish Minister Introducing the Revised Code of Canon Law* (Washington, D. C.: Canon Law Society of America, 1982), p. 32.

4

Freedom to Grow

Janet Gagnon and Patti O'Kane

Freedom is the condition of every human virtue and of every grace. *(Lambeth Conference, 1958)*

"It's not because I was angry or discontented, but there was just more for me in the Episcopal Church." *(Patti O'Kane)*

Baptized membership in the church is a matter of identity, more like belonging to an ethnic group than belonging to a club. But Christians often have difficulty in understanding that difference. The exclusivity of a club is an easier idea to get hold of. If the Daughters of the American Revolution can limit membership to those with the right pedigree and the New York Hibernian Society can decide who is qualified to march down Fifth Avenue on St. Patrick's Day, and a golf club can bounce a member for non-payment of dues, then why, Christians have asked themselves, do we put up with people in our church who don't meet commonly accepted standards of good behavior?

For many churches over the centuries, the answer has been, "We don't. Christian belief should change behavior in ways that are obvious to all." So we find even in the New Testament epistles the beginnings of standards for judging others: children are told to obey their parents and slaves to obey their masters (Col. 3:20-21), and long lists are provided of behavior contrary to the Spirit of Christ, such as "fornication, impurity, licentiousness, idolatry, sorcery, enmities, strife, jealousy, anger, quarrels, dissensions, factions, envy, drunkenness, carousing, and things like these" (Gal. 5:19-21). But even these rules have seemed too easy at times, and so churches have added stricter rules about fasting and going to mass and playing cards and drinking alcoholic beverages and even tea and coffee. Rules like these provide simple ways of passing judgment on who is good and who is bad—though they generally overlook much more harmful behavior such as polluting the atmosphere or creating unemployment and, more importantly, Jesus' own words in the Sermon on the Mount: "Do not judge, so that you may not be judged."

It's frustrating. As members of the body of Christ, as those who see "the glory of the Lord as though reflected in a mirror," we are called to be "transformed into the same image from one degree of glory to another" (2 Cor. 3:18), yet we have found no useful way of measuring and judging who is glorious *enough*. Indeed, we find ourselves forbidden by Christ himself to do so. He told a parable about the servants who wanted to weed their master's garden but were warned not to do it lest they pull up the good plants with the bad. But still we try. Surely we must have some standards!

In our day and age, much of the effort to establish standards for membership has centered in the sexual arena, where Christians have become bitterly divided over divorce, birth control, abortion, and homosexuality. The Roman Catholic Church, in particular, has been deeply divided as papal pronouncements have run counter to the beliefs and practices of a large number of church members. The Episcopal Church, like most other mainline churches today, is not immune from such stress; it, too, has members who want clear rules about right and wrong behavior. But the Anglican tradition of inclusiveness and of giving priority to the pastoral care of individuals still manages—just barely!—to hold the church together and make room for those who might be condemned by a more legalistic system.

Here, then, are two more stories of individuals who came to be incorporated into the Episcopal Church and how, whether they had been comfortable or uncomfortable with the church in which they grew up, they found more room to grow in the Episcopal Church.

He died to take away your sins, not your mind." "There's a difference between being baptized and brainwashed." "There's only one problem with religions that have all the answers. They don't allow questions."

These slogans go with three ads developed by the Church Ad Project, the brainchild of a small group of Episcopalians who thought that people like Colleen Sica had a point: why should the Episcopal Church not proclaim its gifts from the housetops? Over the years they have produced a series of catchy ads that are available to any parish that wants to get some attention. One ad pictures pallbearers carrying a casket into a church and asks "Will it take six strong men to bring you back into the church?" They are wonderful ads and probably very effective at doing what advertising does best: creating a greater and almost subliminal awareness of the product. But how many people are directly moved to come to church because of an ad they saw? When crunch time comes and people are looking for a church, they are more likely to ask a friend.

Janet Kochert and Dennis Gagnon were looking for a church. It wasn't simply a casual search, because they were planning to be married and needed a place for the ceremony. In fact, as so often happens, they had already made plans for a honeymoon cruise in the Caribbean for a particular date in February, and that was less than a year away. But they wanted to be married in church and that presented a problem: both of them were divorced, Dennis was not a church member at all, and Janet was a Roman Catholic.

It was clear to Janet that she, as a divorced person, was a second-class citizen in her church, that it would take time and money to get an annulment. Even if an annulment were forthcoming, she simply didn't believe it should be required of her. Whatever the church might teach, Janet saw things differently. After the divorce she kept going to mass and kept receiving communion. That was important to her and she saw no reason to give it up because she and her husband had come to a parting of the ways. No one said it in so many words, but "they made me feel like I wasn't a full person; as if I had a big red D on my chest." It clearly wouldn't be easy to get permission to remarry after divorce in a church with that attitude. But what alternative did she have? Like most people, she asked around, and her sister had an idea: "Try the Episcopal Church."

How did her sister know? She was married to an Episcopalian. When Janet's sister had her first child, she and her husband had looked at different churches for a baptism and had explored what the Episcopal Church was like. She had liked what she saw: a church very similar to the Roman Catholic Church in many ways, but freer and more open, more democratic. She and her husband never did join a church, but she remembered her impressions of the Episcopal Church. She also knew that her husband's father was divorced and active in an Episcopal church, leading her to believe that maybe Janet would find acceptance too.

So Janet and Dennis set out to explore Episcopal churches along the banks of the Ohio River in southern Indiana. It turned out they had a choice of two, both called St. Paul's: there was St. Paul's Church, New Albany, and St. Paul's Church, Jeffersonville. Starting at Easter time and working through the summer, they visited both churches several times to try to get a feel of each one before deciding. For them it was not simply a matter of which one would look better in wedding pictures: they wanted a church they could belong to, one that would continue to be a part of their lives.

One thing they discovered right away was that Episcopalians were friendly: "They kept coming up to us after the service and inviting us to coffee hour, inviting us back, welcoming us. And that was interesting to me because in the Roman Catholic Church no one would ever have noticed us. The sharing of the Peace had always been uncomfortable there because no one knew anyone." Janet and Dennis declined coffee hour invitations in order to keep their options open, but it was nice to know they would be welcome in either place.

They also knew that Janet, at least, would be welcome to receive communion. The service bulletins made that clear every week. Janet didn't respond to that invitation until they had made a commitment to a church. For one thing, Dennis wasn't baptized so she would have been going to the altar alone; for another, she wasn't sure exactly what she was supposed to do, since the members of these Episcopal churches generally knelt at the altar rail, while she was used to standing in line to receive. So she held back for a while and observed.

Certainly the liturgy was familiar to Janet and not uncomfortable for Dennis. The hard part was that St. Paul's, New Albany, was between rectors and it wasn't clear how things would be when a new rector came. In the end the new rector arrived, but that wasn't what helped them make up their minds. What made the decision was size as much as anything: they liked a smaller congregation, a somewhat less traditional, less formal approach to things, and one, it seemed to both of them, somehow "more related to today." None of this was part of Janet's experience in the Roman Catholic Church, where congregations were large and the liturgies very formal, but she liked it. It felt good. "It felt like it was going to be a church I could be comfortable with." A woman at the altar, on the other hand, had not been part of Janet's experience and here were two churches now with women as rectors. But "I just accepted that real well," she says. "I liked the fact that the Episcopal Church is open enough to ordain women and let a woman do anything a man can do."

So one Sunday they stayed after church and talked to the rector. "We're getting married," they told her, "and we'd like to get married in this church." "I'd love to talk with you," replied the rector, Susan Mills, "about whether you *can* be married in this church." That was a new idea for Janet and Dennis, who were expecting her response would be, "Okay, no problem!" It was a little late to back out, however, and the rector seemed friendly, so they made an appointment to see what would happen next.

Looking back, the Gagnons are amused that they hadn't stopped to think that the Episcopal Church, too, might have some requirements. Janet knows many people who have obtained annulments and she knew all about requirements. In fact, when you talk with her, she seems to have some of her own. She's come to believe, for example, that no one should get married while they are still in school or even before the age of thirty because no one at that stage knows who they really are. Still, there was an initial surprise to find requirements at St. Paul's, but she got over it quickly.

In fact, the number of calls from people wanting to be married at St. Paul's had led the rector and vestry to adopt some definite guidelines—not rules—on the subject. "We want to be welcoming," Susan Mills says, "but we also want them to be really clear that we don't take marriage lightly. I want to find out whether they really want to be part of the Christian community and whether they have a real commitment. I also make it clear that instruction is required; I usually tell them it will be at least six hours, though it often winds up less. But I consider premarital counseling one of the best tools we have for leading people to a deeper understanding and commitment."

Janet and Dennis were quite willing to go with the program. So they began a series of meetings. The rector wanted to explore their relationship, what strengths and weaknesses they would bring to a marriage. She had a questionnaire she used, an inventory of some sort, which they answered separately and then discussed. She also wanted to know about their previous marriage experience. What went wrong? Had they learned from it? Would they do better this time?

"It's a good process," Janet says, looking back. "Her emphasis was on whether we were ready to be married, whether we were right for each other. It wasn't just asking about the past to give us a penance and move on." And Janet had a chance to tell her story.

She had grown up in the Roman Catholic Church and it never occurred to her to be married elsewhere or, most certainly, that she would ever get a divorce. But she got married just after college and it had never really been right. It didn't help that her husband wasn't a Roman Catholic or even a practicing Christian, but the worst part was that somewhere along the line he had lost confidence in himself and it was a strain on their marriage. After college, he went on to graduate school in etymology but didn't do well and was dropped from the program. It seemed to make a change in him and he couldn't get back on track: he took a job in his field but they let him go after a year, then another that didn't last much longer. He started a business on his own, but that didn't go well either. Janet, meanwhile, was doing very well, getting promotions and raises. She traveled a lot and so did her husband, in the effort to get his business off the ground—all of which just made things worse for their relationship.

Clearly it wasn't a great marriage, but all Janet's training said, "If that's how it is, that's how it is." Her parents were still alive and her church's teaching was clear. Divorce was not an option. If her husband's confidence in himself was the problem, perhaps they could work on that. She suggested he go for counseling, but he wasn't interested. She suggested he go back to graduate school and try again. But he didn't want to do that either. It didn't occur to her to look for counseling for herself—though she wishes now that she had—nor did it occur to her to talk with a priest.

In fact, Janet had drifted away from the church herself. Through the college years, she had seldom missed the Sunday mass even if it meant fighting her way through a raging blizzard, but now with an indifferent husband, a failing marriage, and the pressures of a successful career, church had become an occasional thing at best. She did try to make some changes in her life to make things better: she began making a point of arranging her travel for work so that she could be home more at night, even if that meant driving several hours. But nothing seemed to work. And one day, when she came back from a brief holiday with her family, she found that her husband had left. Not long after that he asked for a divorce.

So now, after nine years of marriage, it was time to take charge and make some changes. Janet sold the house, moved to an apartment, and enrolled in an MBA course in a satellite program run by Webster University in St. Louis. The year after that she met Dennis Gagnon, a student in the same program who worked for General Electric in its refrigeration division in Louisville. His division makes about a million refrigerator cases every year. They begin with the raw materials and when they send the cases on, they are ready for the lights and shelves to be installed and finishing touches to be added. Dennis was a team leader of some eighty other employees, helping them to take more responsibility, to be more motivated, to troubleshoot problems, to make sure everything works in the best way possible. Team leadership takes self-confidence and that was what Janet's first husband had lacked.

On the other hand, if her first husband hadn't been a practicing Christian, Dennis wasn't a Christian at all. He had never even been baptized. But he did agree with Janet that they should find a church not only for their wedding but to be a part of their lives. It wasn't that Dennis had no knowledge of Christianity; he had gone to vacation Bible school as a child and enjoyed it. His family wasn't well off, he will tell you, and he liked the free candy and treats that went with the summer programs, but he also valued the sense of commitment he found there. He has very positive memories of the experience and might have looked for a church eventually himself, but Janet made that decision easy.

St. Paul's made it easy too. This was a church with a very definite program. For those who have not been baptized, they have a nine-month catechumenal process that ends with baptism at Easter. Toward the end of September or early October, they have a service for welcoming newcomers, then those who are not already church members begin a program that the parish calls simply "Journey." Janet and Dennis joined a group of about a dozen people, some of them long-time Episcopalians looking for a refresher course but most of them newcomers. St. Paul's takes a faith commitment seriously, and the group meets for an hour or two every Sunday night for six or seven months, until Easter. "I was kind of pulled along into the process," Dennis remembers, "but after we got in, probably I was as enthusiastic as she."

By the time they got involved in that program, they had already had their series of meetings with the rector to prepare for the wedding. Susan Mills remembers that the meetings went very well. Janet already knew a good deal about the faith and since both of them were enrolled in the Journey program, the main agenda of their meetings could be marriage itself and planning the marriage service. There was nevertheless a bit of friction. In the first place, they had scheduled their wedding for the third weekend of February, which on the church calendar was the first Friday in Lent. The church has a long tradition of no weddings in Lent except for good and sufficient reason, a requirement that hadn't occurred to either Janet or Dennis when they made their plans. When they told Susan Mills about it, "It didn't sit well with her," they said, but cruises are hard to reschedule and she was willing to go along with them. "She's a pretty contemporary kind of person," according to Janet, "but in some things she's pretty strict." There were rules about the kind of music you could have and taking pictures was forbidden during the service, but if Susan could bend the rule about weddings in Lent, Dennis and Janet could get along with the other rules. So the wedding took place on schedule.

Or almost on schedule. The wedding was scheduled for Friday and on Thursday there was a major blizzard, eight to ten inches of new snow on a region not used to that sort of thing. The whole area was paralyzed. The rector called to discuss how to handle the situation and Janet heard Dennis saying, "Okay, cancel it!" She was frantic thinking of the food they had bought, the money already spent, but it turned out Dennis was talking about the rehearsal. There was no way people could get to the church that night, so the rehearsal was rescheduled for Friday, right before the service itself. At least that way there was no time for them to forget what to do! Half the invited guests never did get there, but for those who did the joy of the occasion was only heightened by the sense of a further obstacle overcome.

When they came back from their honeymoon cruise, they could concentrate better on the Journey process. At St. Paul's those who, like Dennis, are unbaptized are enrolled as candidates on the first Sunday in Lent, writing their names in a book to make it clear they have really signed up for something. Candidates for baptism are given sponsors, too: usually a man and a woman of similar age and interests who can tell the candidate out of their own experience what it means to be a follower of Jesus Christ. Dennis's baptism at the Easter Vigil service, celebrated at 6 a.m. on Easter Day, more than made up for the weeks of preparation and going without communion. If he had been on the sidelines before, now he, as the only adult being baptized, was the center of attention at the most important service of the year. It was "pretty exciting," he remembers. There was a champagne brunch afterwards and now Dennis was definitely part of the community. As for Janet, she would have been received when the bishop came in May, but a business trip came up and she couldn't be there. She had to wait until fall to be officially welcomed into the community.

But neither Janet nor Dennis had any doubt that they were welcome. Dennis, in fact, was so thoroughly welcomed that before he knew it, he was on the vestry—and not only on the vestry, but a warden besides, less than a year from his baptism! Is that normal at St. Paul's? "It was a very special case," Susan Mills explains. "We had a personality situation on the vestry that was creating real problems and we needed someone just at that point with the skills Dennis had. He's kind of laid back and has a good sense of humor, but he also has management skills. I would get really tense and he would relieve the tension."

But Dennis, laid back or not, was not happy with the situation. In the first place, "It seemed like I went from not attending to attending to being on the vestry, and I did feel a little uncomfortable." Besides that, it was a position that needed more time than he could give. He was working ten- and twelve-hour days and there was not time to do his job, build a new marriage, and give the parish the kind of leadership it needed. "Susan was happy with the job I was doing, but I wasn't. If I couldn't do it right, I didn't want to do it." He resigned after less than a year. But that was enough: he had helped the parish get across a critical transition. For one thing, the personality problems in the vestry had been resolved and the whole atmosphere of the parish had changed. "I wouldn't do it today," says the rector, "because now it's a totally different vestry and a totally different parish." But Dennis was there when he was needed.

Of course, when you join a small parish you will get asked to take on responsibilities. Jeffersonville is a funny mix of small town and sophisticated suburb. It's just a few minutes across the bridge to Louisville, with its symphony orchestra, art galleries, jobs, and good restaurants. People live in New Albany and Jeffersonville because it is less expensive and they can have the advantages both of the small town where everybody knows everybody and the city with its cosmopolitan community. But a small parish in a small town will still have difficulties finding leadership and needs everyone to give a hand.

Janet was asked to serve on the finance committee; she accepted, but after one meeting she realized she was overcommitted and resigned. It seems to her that perhaps the parish pushes too hard, especially on newcomers, and there's a danger of burnout. Janet prefers to take her time and not get in any further than she knows she can handle. For the time being, she serves as a greeter and just likes being part of the community. Dennis serves as a lay reader, taking a turn every month or two. "I'm used to talking to large groups," he points out, "so I feel good about doing that." He is happy too that his seventeen-year-old daughter from his first marriage comes to church with them. "I guess I view church as just part of having a good life," Dennis sums it up. And when he thinks about what his marriage and his church have brought into his life, he adds, "I feel like I'm doubly blessed."

In the days of the Roman Empire it was said that "all roads lead to Rome." No one would claim that all roads today lead into the Episcopal Church, but certainly there are many that do. Steve Roman and Tony Merlo found two very different roads and Patti O'Kane found still another. Like Steve Roman, Patti was not looking for a new church, and like him, she had a very real loyalty to the Church of Rome. Patti O'Kane knows a thing or two about being loyal to the church. She learned it from her parents growing up in a faithful Roman Catholic home, but she was thirty years old before her father let her know how deeply his loyalty had once been tested.

"I was twelve years old," John O'Kane told his daughter, "and I had gone to play handball with my father. In the middle of the game he had a massive heart attack and his first thought was to send for the priest. He told me to run to the church and get the priest to come. So I ran to the church and gave the priest the message, but he refused to come. I begged him. I told him my father was dying. He said, 'You're insolent,' and he slapped me and closed the door. So I ran back to the handball court and found that my father was dead."

An experience like that, you can easily imagine, might turn some people against the church, but not Mr. O'Kane. "There is original sin," he explained to his daughter, "and priests are human beings too. I can't blame that on the church."

John O'Kane, who served as a police officer and then as a professor of criminal justice at a small community college, still loves the church and his daughter inherited that love. The church was the center of her life in Uniondale, a middle-class community on Long Island. Her parish, St. Martha's, was youth-oriented and a great place for kids. As Patti moved up through the parochial school and a diocesan high school there was always something going on at the church or the school and Patti was often in the middle of it. She was deeply involved in the Catholic Youth Organization, the CYO, and loved athletics. In the sixties the government was trying to get Americans to exercise, so Patti exercised—and won four presidential awards for physical fitness. She also learned to play the guitar, joined a folk group, and played for masses. When Pope John XXIII came to Madison Square Garden, Patti was there behind him playing her guitar.

But for all the satisfaction and support she found, there was something that seemed not quite right. When her friends began to date, Patti found herself feeling like an outsider. "Whatever relationships I had, I didn't feel good about; they didn't seem to lead anywhere. I began to wonder if I was capable of a deep relationship with anyone." Besides that doubt, she began to realize that for her sexual attraction was usually to women. One therapist she went to said, "You'll grow out of it," but finally she found one who helped her come to terms with her identity and develop the confidence in herself that would make deeper relationships possible.

To say that Patti O'Kane's sexuality shaped her life is to say only what is true of every human being. But the sexuality of most people inclines them toward marriage and producing children, and it also inclines them to be suspicious of or hostile toward those whose sexuality does not. Both the Roman Catholic and Episcopal churches have condemned such hostility, but the very fact that they have had to do so indicates something of the difficulty homosexual people have in recognizing who they are and being open about it to others. Inevitably, that difference shapes their lives, and so it was with Patti. The thoughts she had of being a nun, for example, were put aside for fear that her sexual orientation would be discovered and she would be rejected. It shaped her choice of a career; eventually, it would shape her church life also.

Putting aside thoughts of the convent, Patti went instead to a two-year community college and then a school of nursing. She liked science and medicine and thought nursing would be a way to develop those interests. But in the science courses she learned something else about herself: that she was not good at lab work. She couldn't draw blood or do the technical things nurses have to do; one instructor told her openly in front of the class that she would never make it. That was a challenge, and Patti, as usual, responded to it: she could at least do what she had to do. But she was better with people. She was good at interviews and assessments. Working with another nurse who had skills with the test tube and needle, she made half of a great team. And when she discovered psychiatric nursing, she had found a career. She went on to earn a master's degree specializing in nursing education.

Degrees firmly in hand, Patti O'Kane launched out into the world of nursing. The Down State Medical Center in Brooklyn gave her her first job as a nurse and her first experience with poverty and mental illness, but not with psychiatric nursing, which was what she really wanted. That opportunity came six years later with a position in the child psychiatry outpatient program at Brookdale Hospital Medical Center in East New York, a section of Brooklyn dominated by an Orthodox Jewish community and a West Indian community. You don't have to work in a New York hospital long to see about all there is to see of human life. Not everyone could survive the daily round of shootings, stabbings, drug-induced psychoses, and other trauma, but Patti loved the challenge and the chance to make a difference.

The church was still at the center of her life and there were still many opportunities to get involved. The Diocese of Brooklyn was a relatively liberal place in those days, exploring the new liturgical freedom that resulted from Vatican II and working hard to include the laity. It wasn't hard to find a parish that would welcome her and give her a role to play. She became a lector and valued the chance it gave her to meet with other members and share their experience of faith.

But some things she couldn't yet share with her faith community. Prejudice and anger and misinformation swirl around the subject of homosexual identity, so it is often easier to avoid the subject and keep that part of yourself hidden. Few people find it easy to talk about their sexuality under the best of circumstances, but if talking about it may cost you your friends, your job, even the love and acceptance of your parents—and none of this is uncommon—it is easy to see why the challenge is often more than those involved can face. Eventually, it was a psychologist she was dating, someone who was not even a Christian, who pushed Patti to come out and to go to a meeting of Dignity, the Roman Catholic association for gays and lesbians.

That first step was hard, but Patti had always been given strong support by her family and her church, so finally one day she went to a meeting of the Brooklyn chapter. There were perhaps a dozen people present and one of them was John McNeill, a Jesuit who had written and spoken frequently on the subject of homosexuality. That was the meeting at which he broke a ten-year silence to declare himself openly for the first time, an act that led to his expulsion from the Jesuit order. Others at the meeting, however, were far from open about themselves. Most of them, as Patti remembers it, were school teachers and very worried about losing their jobs if their sexual identity were discovered.

The little group welcomed Patti warmly and helped her get over her initial anxiety, but not much was happening there. It was simply a pleasant social gathering. These were not people prepared to face the world and declare themselves. Patti O'Kane, on the other hand, is an activist. She likes to make things happen. Once she began to feel comfortable with who she was, the Brooklyn Dignity chapter wasn't enough to keep her interested. Someone suggested she try a meeting of Integrity, an organization describing itself as "a gay and lesbian justice ministry in and to the Episcopal Church."

And so it came about that Patti crossed the East River one day and went to a meeting of Integrity. An old Episcopal church in Greenwich Village, St. Luke's in the Fields, has hosted the New York chapter of Integrity for many years. It's a large group and involved in numerous activities. They welcomed her warmly to her first meeting in May and before the summer was over they put her on a committee. Someone was needed to serve on the committee for the National AIDS memorial, and who better than the newest member?

The people at Integrity couldn't have known it, but they had made an inspired choice. Patti O'Kane is a doer who always seems to be able to take on something more. But more important, she was just beginning to move into AIDS work as a career. And that, too, came about because Patti O'Kane, encouraged by her new support group but gifted also with the security family and church can provide, is willing to speak up when she has something to say. The *New York Times* had run a series of articles on the AIDS crisis, sending a reporter into bars and gathering places in Manhattan to see whether people were well informed about the nature of AIDS and the resources available. By and large, the reporter learned, there were lots of resources and people were well aware of them. Patti thought, "That's all very well on the east side of Manhattan, where people are generally well educated and the resources are abundant, but what about my community?"

So Patti sat down and wrote a letter to the *Times*. There are, she pointed out, communities where there is a lot more fear than facts, a lot more rumors than resources. "Take Brookdale Hospital, for example," she wrote. Here was a hospital surrounded by two communities so intolerant of homosexuality that the hospital had been afraid to face up to the need. "What about places like these," she asked, "where there is no education and there are no options and where institutions are afraid to do what is needed?"

Patti's friends were aghast. Who, after all, would write a letter to the *Times* criticizing her employer unless she had private means or a deep desire to seek new employment? Fearing the hospital's reaction and the consequences to Patti, her friends called to ask if they could help her find a new job. But the Spirit who moved Patti to write the letter was, as usual, working out a plan. Yes, the hospital had been fearful of moving too fast in this area, but unbeknownst to her they had applied for and received a grant to create an AIDS unit and were waiting for the right moment to move ahead. Clearly, if they were being held up as a bad example for the whole city to see, the right moment had come to proceed with the plan. And if the hospital was to have an AIDS unit, why not let Patti O'Kane help develop it? So instead of finding herself out on the street regretting her impulsive nature, she found herself suddenly working with a psychologist to create a new hospital unit in order to begin a whole new ministry.

She found herself with another new ministry as well. If being fearless could create a new hospital unit and transform her career, perhaps it could make a difference for others. Certainly there were other issues that needed to be addressed. The constant diet of pro-life letters in Roman Catholic newspapers, in particular, seemed to Patti to express a moral blindness that was wrong for Christians. So she began to write letters, first to *The Long Island Catholic*:

> If this pro-life movement was really pro-life, it would not stand in the way of programs for poor women that supply birth control and prevent pregnancy. Pro-lifers should spend a week living in the projects where I practice nursing (Brownsville, Brooklyn) rather than congratulating themselves for a night in jail. Come see the ravages of poverty, drugs, classism, and discrimination firsthand.... Come meet a pregnant, drug-abusing mother with three children who is HIV positive. Why doesn't the pro-life movement muster its talents to get this mother drug treatment, adequate pre-natal care and, yes,

birth control.... The doctors and nurses of my hospital invite you to take and change the streets here in East New York, Brownsville, Bed-Stuy, etc. I'm tired of implications that doctors and nurses who don't agree with you aren't pro-life.

Perhaps also Patti was beginning to acquire a new theological slant on some of these issues, and to see them in terms of the church's orientation toward questions that tend to polarize Christian theologians: theology stressing the fall and redemption on the one hand, and creation and incarnation on the other. Anglican theologians have tended to emphasize the latter, Roman Catholics and evangelicals the former. Patti's letters were beginning to have an incarnational ring, as in this one to the Brooklyn diocesan newspaper, *The Tablet*:

Fall-redemption theology has a self-righteousness to it that glories in feeling entitled to denigrate others while failing to respond to the social, psychological, and medical needs of those the finger is pointed at. This punitive, constantly castigating theology is what is killing the church.

How can children come to believe and trust us about issues of respect and responsibility when so little respect is given to people with AIDS and when their health care predicament is translated into a moral quagmire rather than a human dilemma?.... Maybe the goal is to transform our lives through acts of corporate mercy rather than stand apart from others and judge, label and stigmatize them further. Love will be the product of their endeavor, not burnout. The hardest part is welcoming into our churches people who have this virus and embracing them at our coffee hours.

Perhaps Patti was beginning to wonder whether she was sitting in the right pew when she wrote to the same paper later that year, "I would like to be a member of a church that did something for teenagers already infected by this virus rather than a church that opted for ideology over people's lives."

In fact, church membership was becoming an issue that Patti would have to face. Except for that, the various aspects of her life seemed to be coming together: first, Integrity had given her a support group and resource for whom AIDS was a major issue, and then the hospital had made AIDS the center of her professional career as well. But now she had two churches, since by belonging to Integrity she had learned something about the Episcopal Church and gotten involved in it to some degree. She hadn't expected that to be a problem since she had a church with which she was happy, and for Patti, as for many Roman Catholics, there were Catholics and there were Protestants, and that was all you needed to know. The Roman Catholic Church had the sacraments and the liturgy and the pope and Protestants didn't. Specialists might be able to tell a Baptist from a Lutheran and an Episcopalian from a Congregationalist, but why would an ordinary Roman Catholic care? Patti walked into St. Luke's and saw no statues, no votive lights, a severely plain colonial building, and wrote it off as one more Protestant church.

But it did have a liturgy. The monthly meetings of Integrity had three parts: eucharist, speaker, and social time. The liturgy came first and, to her surprise, it was wonderfully familiar. So maybe she was wrong about Protestants and maybe the Episcopal Church was not as different from the Roman Catholic Church as she had thought. But there was one difference: in this liturgy, women were taking roles never assigned to them in her church. So how did she as a faithful Roman Catholic feel about all that? "Did I think I was in the wrong place? No, I felt lied to. Did I think I would go to hell if I participated? No, I thought I was in heaven." But still, however similar it might be, there is such a thing as loyalty. Even when the priest slaps you in the face, you don't turn against the church. And Patti O'Kane had certainly not been slapped in the face. On the contrary, she was a valued member of her parish with an honored part to play in the liturgy. And why would you leave a church where you were comfortable and happy?

So Patti O'Kane went to the meetings of Integrity and continued to serve as before in her parish in Brooklyn. And Integrity continued to put new opportunities in her way. Would she serve as regional vice-president, for example? "But remember," she told them, "I'm a Roman Catholic." "So?" they replied. This was not the attitude toward church membership Patti had been brought up with, but she liked it. She became regional vice-president, and when the 1991 General Convention came along she was there to help represent the organization.

General Convention was an education in itself. The convention center was filled with booths representing every advocacy group in the church—and some not in the church. There were forums almost daily at which those with various agendas could push them. No one could possibly take it all in. But Integrity knew how to play the game and make sure their views were heard. Scholars like Professor John Boswell of Yale, an expert on the role of homosexuality in the Middle Ages, spoke at an Integrity forum and bishops sat in the audience to listen. This was not like the Roman Catholic Church as Patti had known it, and she came home with a lot to think about.

The more deeply Patti became involved in Integrity, the more she was drawn into other services and meetings in which the Episcopal Church was on display. She was beginning to feel very comfortable with what she found. "The theology was the same and the sacraments were the same," she realized. "I felt at home." But she continued to discover differences as well; in the Episcopal Church Patti O'Kane saw things she had never seen at home. On St. Francis' Day, she went to the Cathedral of St. John the Divine and there was an elephant being led in procession up the center aisle. Patti had never seen an elephant in the aisle before. "In the Roman Church," she remembered, "they would come to the door and bless nature outside, but here in the Episcopal Church they were rolling it up the aisle!"

More important, that was the day she found herself sitting behind two women who were obviously a couple and clearly in love. There was nothing flamboyant about them, just a quiet warmth and affection that Patti couldn't help observing. These were people who were comfortable with themselves and had no need to flaunt it. Patti found that very liberating. "It was no longer something to be ashamed of, not simply okay—it was something good."

That realization, in turn, undoubtedly helped deepen a developing relationship with a new friend from Integrity. Brooke Bushong, unlike Patti, was a lifelong Episcopalian. Indeed, she was a member of the Church Army, a worldwide Anglican organization somewhat similar to the Salvation Army, which trains church members to work as evangelists in areas of special need. Church Army officers serve in inner city, rural, Native American, and overseas missions, as well as in parish and institutional settings. Brooke had worked with migrant laborers in California and on the staff of Covenant House, rescuing homeless teenagers from the sexual predators around Times Square in Manhattan. At first, she seemed rather cold and indifferent, but one evening a small group went out together after an Integrity meeting and Patti began to see something more behind the quiet and unassuming exterior. Introvert and extrovert, lifelong Episcopalian and newcomer from Rome, different in almost every way, the two women found themselves recognizing an extraordinary compatibility. Now registered with New York City as domestic partners, they hope one day for the Episcopal Church to give its approval of same-sex unions so they can ask God's blessing on their relationship.

It was Brooke who brought Patti to St. Clement's Church, in the Times Square area of Manhattan. You can find almost any kind of Episcopal Church you might want in Manhattan: the smoke-filled solemnity of St. Mary the Virgin a few blocks away, the drum and guitar-supported evangelical fervor of All Angels' a few blocks north, the rather English elegance of St. Thomas Fifth Avenue, with its famous boys' choir a bit north and east, the patrician simplicity of St. James', Madison Avenue—there's something for almost everybody and you don't have to go far to find it. But most people would still not find St. Clement's.

Walk west from Times Square far enough, to an area of dingy brick walk-ups, and you will walk right past the dingy bricks of St. Clement's unless you are paying close attention. Buzz hard at the reinforced metal door; this is a neighborhood where not even the church can safely have an open door policy. Once inside, don't look for oak pews and a distant altar because for most of the week, St. Clement's is an off-Broadway theater.

When Sunday comes, they move things around a bit and it becomes a church in the midst of the stage settings and props. Here a stalwart band of Christians gathers weekly to celebrate a liturgy which probably satisfies none of them entirely. They work on it constantly, changing this and trying that and hoping some day—possibly but not necessarily before the Second Coming—that they will get it right at last. There is, for example, something called the "Mother Thunder Liturgy" (James and John, you might remember were the "Sons of Thunder") and sometime in the past, no one quite remembers when, they even developed their own creed. Patti and Brooke would prefer the Nicene Creed—which is also used on occasion—but this is a feisty community and you can't always get your own way. There is, however, a combination of informality and tradition that Patti likes. She finds that the stark surroundings help her see the church more as a gathering around a holy table. She's learned to be less critical of the fine points of liturgy and more focused on the central action through which the community comes to life.

Focus is important at St. Clement's because it's not always clear whether the church is there for the theater or the theater is there for the church. And in such a neighborhood, the people who come through the door may need more attention than the ordinary parish might be able to give. "Is it substance abuse?" asks Patti. "We're used to it. Is it mental illness? We can handle it." So maybe it isn't a church that conforms in every detail to the requirements of the *Book of Common Prayer* and the genteel traditions of a suburban parish, but this is a church on the frontline and allowances may need to be made.

With this additional exposure to and experience of the Episcopal Church, Patti went again to General Convention in 1994, and now she was in the thick of things. Just as Integrity has an agenda, so also do other church groups. If Integrity is lobbying for a particular resolution or canon, there is probably another group somewhere else lobbying against it. There were working breakfasts, lunch meetings, forums, committee hearings, chance encounters in the corridors. But perhaps more important, there were opportunities for Patti and members of Integrity to let people meet them and see them not as stereotypes but as ordinary, hardworking, faithful people not so different after all from those you might meet on Main Street or in the parish hall back home.

Each day of Convention began with a eucharist and everyone was assigned a table where they would gather day by day with a dozen assorted church members: perhaps a bishop from Mississippi, a housewife from Nicaragua, an executive from Chicago, a store owner from a small town in Iowa, a priest from Fort Worth. At Patti's table was the director of a group campaigning against Integrity's agenda; he was quite friendly and polite. "It changes people," Patti has learned, " to see normal people taking part in the life of the church and not flaunting anything."

Patti came back to New York pondering the fact that she had talked one-on-one or in small groups with at least twenty bishops—"and in the Roman Catholic Church," she thought to herself, "about the closest I've been is to see one walk up the aisle in a procession!" How could she not join a church that had taken her so seriously? It seemed to her she had no real alternative. So she joined an inquirers' class at St. Clement's Church and was received into the Episcopal Church at the Cathedral of St. John the Divine. "I couldn't remain divided. It's not because I was angry or discontented, but there was just more for me in the Episcopal Church. I saw that as a lay person—as an 'out' gay person —I could have an influence." Indeed, she could; it wasn't long before St. Clement's needed a new rector and Patti found herself in charge of the search committee, faced with the almost impossible task of finding a priest able to live with so diverse a community and give it new impetus and coherence.

Growing steadily more comfortable with her own identity and with the Episcopal Church, Patti began finding ways to include the church in her work. She was putting her training in nursing education to use by guiding nursing students from New York University in their practicum, providing them with the practical experience and exposure that the students needed in the field of community nursing. A field trip to Holy Apostles' Church in the Hell's Kitchen area of Manhattan, for example, seemed to be a good way to integrate several types of experience and show them a model of community organizations working together. Here, where the biggest soup kitchen in the city feeds hundreds of people every day, the students could watch as homeless and hungry people with all kinds of disabilities were ministered to, with the church right there in the background.

"Nurses," Patti says, "don't usually see the church as part of the picture. Their only contact with the church comes when they pull the sheet over a dead patient and put in a call for the chaplain." But at Holy Apostles they can see the Rev. Liz Maxwell discussing a client with the nurse and doctor who set up shop in a trailer on the street outside the church. People too paranoid or psychotic or drunk or simply fearful of authority to come to a standard health facility can come here and be helped. And the student nurses, away from the hospital and their often limited neighborhoods, could see people in their own environment who might be their patients some day.

Patti realizes that without the Episcopal Church to support her, she would not have taken the student nurses there. Why not? "If you're not worried about people telling you what you can do and how you should think, you can be more creative. It's a control issue. The Roman Church has to control things. The Episcopal Church leaves you free to work things out for yourself." And Patti has a lot to work out: "I'm working with criminals, people with sickle cell anemia, children with AIDS. You name it, I've seen it. People tell me," she adds, "that my AIDS work is a vocation. If it is, it's because the Episcopal Church has nourished it."

And from her vantage point in the Episcopal Church, she has gained a new perspective on the Roman Catholicism with which she grew up and which still keeps the loyalty of her parents. Her mother taught her to love the rosary and she still uses it. She still likes to see some statues—although there are limits, and she refers to her parents' parish as "Disneyland." Patti still subscribes to Roman Catholic magazines and newspapers and writes to them to let them know that there are other viewpoints. When a bishop teaching in the New York archdiocesan seminary described AIDS as "a punishment for sin," it was important to her to write a letter and express another opinion. People need to have another viewpoint put in front of them, even if only to make them aware that they are not alone—or that their views are not unchallenged. She sees a "split personality" in the Roman Catholic Church: freedom and generosity in some areas, such as care for the poor and the hungry, but on issues of sexuality and gender, she sees only rigidity, with no room for alternative views.

Patti has strong views and she can put them starkly, but more often her pleading is for compassion, understanding, and patience. The possibility that gay activists would publicly reveal the names of closeted homosexuals, including bishops, inspired a letter to the editor recommending that they first go read Matthew 18: "If another member of the church sin against you, go and point out the fault when the two of you are alone." When a pastor writing in the *American Journal of Nursing* urged that children be told the truth if they are dying, she wrote to warn clergy against pushing their agenda on parents prematurely: "More often than not, parents need time to adjust to the bad news and require prepared support to find the words to speak the truth." She has similar concerns about HIV testing at too early a stage: "The clinician must be able to delay her own urgency to know while gently supporting the patient's denial and lack of readiness. Timing is essential if the patient is to both cope with bad news and enter into the partnership of a treatment plan."

That kind of sensitivity to people can wear thin under the pressures of hospital work in the inner city. Patti O'Kane knows that full well and has found ways to keep her balance. Birds are a hobby and her letters have appeared in several bird and wildlife magazines. Currently she is involved in a correspondence with experts on the possibility that a rare pulmonary virus might be transmitted by handling owl pellets, which many conservation centers do in order to learn about the habits of owls. Thus her technical knowledge of viruses proves valuable even in her leisure time pursuits!

A nursing magazine ran a feature on Patti that showed her holding a little boy in her right arm while a large black-faced sheep leaned over her left shoulder to eat out of the boy's outstretched hand. The accompanying article explains that she spends a part of every other Sunday at the Bronx Zoo as a docent, part of a volunteer corp, introducing children to the wonders of the animal kingdom. "I need to spend my time off," she is quoted as saying, "where there is new life and children filled with hope."

But surely new life is what her work in the hospital is all about as well, and new life is what she has found in the Episcopal Church.

Precisely because so many people come searching for a church that seems better able to live with some ambiguity in the sexual arena, something needs to be said about the Anglican way of dealing with these issues. In the first place, any official statements made by the Episcopal Church have been adopted by a General Convention in which lay people have an equal voice with clergy. In the second place, the whole tradition of the Anglican Communion, of which the Episcopal Church is only a part, is more concerned with a pastoral approach than one based on law.

So, for example, faced with the question of remarriage after divorce, the Episcopal Church relies primarily on the pastoral judgment of the parish priest who meets with the couple, forms on opinion of their readiness to marry, and then requests the bishop's approval. Such reliance on the judgment of individual priests makes for some variety from one parish to the next; a couple might be turned away in one parish and welcomed in another. But that seems preferable, most Episcopalians would agree, to a system that prohibits all remarriage after divorce and then creates a legal loophole by making most marriages susceptible to "annulment."

These are difficult issues. Few people can be comfortable with the number of marriages ending in divorce or the number of pregnancies ending in abortion. Some would suggest that these statistics suggest a need for new laws and restrictions, but others see it as evidence of our need to learn how to make responsible use of our freedom. One of the best statements on this subject was issued by the gathering of Anglican bishops held every ten years called the Lambeth Conference:

Freedom is the condition of every human virtue and of every grace,...the way towards the attainment of all that is excellent and true. And, perplexing though the choices in contemporary marriage are, it must also be said that the new freedom of sexuality in marriage in our time is also, and equally, a gate into a new depth and joy in personal relationships between husband and wife. At a time when so much in our culture tends to depersonalize life—to erode and dissolve the old, clear, outlines of human personality—Christians may well give thanks for the chance to establish in marriage a new level of intimate, loving interdependence between husband and wife and parents and children, freed from some of the old disciplines of fear.

It must be said at once that this will not happen automatically. It will happen only when we deliberately choose it, and pay the cost of it in self-discipline, in courtesy toward one another within the marital tie, and the willingness to receive and give the fullest communication of love, physically as well as in every other way.[1]

What the bishops said about marriage is true of all human relationships. Freedom involves risks, but we can become mature, responsible human beings only by being allowed to take the risk of freedom. St. Paul wrote, "For freedom Christ has set us free. Stand firm, therefore, and do not submit again to a yoke of slavery" (Gal. 5:1).

Notes

1. *The Lambeth Conference, 1958* (London: SPCK, 1958).

5

Authority and Freedom

John Mulryan and Jerry Gallagher

"We didn't learn much about the Episcopal Church that I can remember, but we learned it was open and accepting and tolerated ambiguity." *(John Mulryan)*

"God's work is always more wonderful than our human models and structures. It's a mistake to take them too seriously. We need to do our thinking inductively, as God does, and bring out what's best in the culture. I love the way the Anglican Church takes human history seriously." *(Jerry Gallagher)*

Dear Pope Paul...." Father Gallagher was writing a letter to the pope. It was the hardest letter he had ever had to write and, as he wrote, his thoughts went back to the days when he, as a seminarian, had actually met the pope:

When you visited us at our Villa in Castelgondolfo eight years ago, you gave each of us a book you had written. We were all very happy to see you and to experience the warmth that brought extra life to the words you wrote. In your homily on the life of John Vianney, your description of the meaning of being a priest has rung true beautifully in my own priestly ministry these past five years....In trying to be close to people and share Christ's love with them, their trust and love has deepened my faith and made my daily thanksgiving for the gift of life much richer.

Jerry Gallagher loved being a priest. It was, as he told the pope, the fulfillment of dreams that had developed in a very natural way over many years, "all I had hoped for and more. I absolutely loved parish work."

Parish work for Jerry Gallagher had begun when he was ordained and assigned to the Church of St. Jerome in the Flatbush section of Brooklyn, a solidly middle-class neighborhood little different from the section of Queens from which he came. The pastor was an auxiliary bishop and there were four priests to share in the work of a parish of five thousand families. A priest could sit all day in the rectory simply dealing with those who came in and have more than enough to do, but Jerry Gallagher walked the streets and called on people in their homes. "What are you doing that for?" one of his fellow priests asked him. Jerry mumbled something about "Jesus' example." The other priest was outraged. "What's that got to do with it?" he asked. "Jesus wasn't a diocesan priest."

But Jerry Gallagher had the idea that there was a relationship between the two and he continued to try to be with people as he thought that Jesus had, and it made him sensitive to the struggles of so many of them to be faithful Catholics as their church defined it. In particular, it was a struggle to abide by the church's teaching about birth control and at the same time provide properly for a family. Children are expensive; clothes and food cost money. But children also need love and enormous amounts of time and sometimes those demands come in conflict with the relationship between a husband and a wife who find themselves, between work and children, with too little time for each other. Jerry Gallagher especially remembers a friend of his who was married and had six children in seven years.

That familiarity with the way ordinary people lived led before long to a crisis in his ministry. He had been there just a week and a half when a document called *Humanae Vitae* was issued. "Well," said one of the clergy at dinner that night, "that settles it." "Settles what?" asked the brash young priest who had just been added to the staff. "Settles the question about birth control," replied the priest. "The pope has finally spoken and that settles it." In the old days, it would also have concluded the dinner table discussion, but Fr. Gallagher, educated in Rome though he was, had apparently absorbed a different attitude toward authority on the streets of Brooklyn and Queens. He found himself holding forth for fifteen minutes on the theological difficulties with the papal statement and the reasons why the statement did not, in fact, settle the issue for him. "It was clear that it wasn't right," he remembers thinking. "I was saddened by the reality—the practical consequences of the pope's statement."

The head pastor, needless to say, was neither pleased nor persuaded but the discussion definitely did clarify his thinking about the new assistant priest. "I can't have someone disloyal to the pope in this parish," he said. Shortly thereafter Jerry Gallagher found himself transferred to the Church of St. Clement Pope, a small black parish in South Ozone Park, a church in a poor neighborhood directly under the flight path to John F. Kennedy airport. Whatever future Jerry Gallagher may have had in the church was clearly under a substantial cloud. "But I didn't care," he says, "because *Humanae Vitae* was a denigration of married love and I knew it was wrong."

There was a time when papal authority went largely unquestioned in American Roman Catholic parishes. Perhaps it was the fact that so many church members were recent immigrants and valued the unity and support the church gave them in their struggle to establish themselves in a new world; perhaps it was the fact that there was in those days little if any conflict between the pope's values and their own. Large families had always been an asset; women did not question their role as homemakers and caregivers; effective methods of birth control were not available anyway. So if the pope was opposed to birth control, it made no practical difference to their lives.

But by the time Jerry Gallagher was ordained the world had changed, and large families were no longer desirable: the material and psychological costs were too great. Opportunities opening up for education and travel and material possessions didn't fit with large families and, even more important, opportunities were appearing for husbands and wives to share leisure time in new ways and to grow together into a richer marital relationship. Now when the pope spoke, it meant significant sacrifice; it meant the loss of those values which seemed to Jerry Gallagher and many others to be completely consistent with Jesus' teaching.

The problem of authority is probably the most important single issue facing American Roman Catholics today. It has been a great strength of the Church of Rome that it could speak clearly and decisively on vital issues, but when the voice of a church seems to have lost touch with the needs and concerns of its members, when it seems, in fact, to have lost touch with the meaning of the gospel for the world we live in, then that strength becomes instead a source of conflict and weakness. Jerry Gallagher in Brooklyn was not the only priest whose ministry was driven into crisis by *Humanae Vitae*: Jerry Lamb, reading that same document in Denver, knew he could no longer function effectively as a priest.

In Manhattan another Roman Catholic priest, John Mulryan, also knew he had a problem when he received a summary of *Humanae Vitae* from the archdiocese with instructions to read it from the pulpit on a certain Sunday. "I had no doubt about reading it," he recalls, "because people had a right to know what the pope had said, but it was customary for the priest reading an official statement to add his own comments of approval and exhortation. That I could not do. I read the statement and simply turned in the pulpit and walked away. The silence was audible. It was the only way I could show my disagreement—and it was clear what I was saying."

Even now, twenty-five years later, John Mulryan's normally quiet voice takes on a note of passion as he recalls the moment. "I felt it was immoral. It was wrong. I had learned a style of theology and a way of thinking theologically and *Humanae Vitae* didn't square with it. And besides that, I had heard so many confessions of people struggling with too many children and practicing birth control. It was putting women in a bind where they had no workable alternative to going through life feeling sinful."

But what can you do when you belong to a church whose chief authority is said to be infallible and that authority has ordered obedience? Ordinary church members may be able to ignore those teachings they are unable to accept—and that is what many have done. The term "cafeteria Catholic" was invented to describe the pattern of behavior adopted by many who have learned to pick and choose what teaching they will follow and what they will disregard. Many lay members of the church seem comfortable with that situation and consider themselves good church members—but on their terms, not the pope's. Others, either because they cannot live with that kind of tension or because they have been divorced and want to remarry, look for alternatives.

Clergy, however, are in a more difficult position. If papal teaching requires them to impose burdens on church members which they are unwilling to impose, their choice is between direct and indirect disobedience on the one hand, and leaving the ministry to which they have been called on the other.

Jerry Gallagher and John Mulryan are two priests who experienced significant difficulties with the Roman Catholic Church because of the dilemma they faced when the pope ruled against artificial means of birth control. Although they are only a few years apart in age and grew up within a few miles of each other in New York City, one in the Bronx, the other in Brooklyn, they have met only in passing. Their stories, similar in some ways but quite different in others, help to illustrate the differences between the Roman and Anglican ways of dealing with the issue of authority.

Americans today look back on the 1950s as a sunlit era of peace and prosperity, but the reality was rather different. It included, among other things, a brutal war in Korea, an obsession with Communism that culminated in the paranoia of the McCarthy era, and the beginnings of the civil rights movement with the dispatch of troops to Little Rock, Arkansas, to force a governor to accept the authority of the Supreme Court. But in the neighborhoods that later made "Archie Bunker" a synonym for narrow-minded bigotry, who would question a pattern that has given security to you and opportunity to your children? Jerry Gallagher's parents were first-generation Americans of Polish and Irish stock; America had been good to their parents and to them.

As for the Roman Catholic Church of Jerry Gallagher's youth, it seemed to be all that a church should be: solid, faithful, sure. The church was not simply part of the very texture of life, but the central institution that gave meaning to all the others. The Holy Cross brothers who taught in the high school Jerry attended provided highly attractive role models for their students. Their happiness impressed Jerry Gallagher deeply and he felt that he wanted to join them and teach others as they had taught him. When he graduated from high school he entered their novitiate, but a six-month term there was enough to persuade him that his true calling was to priesthood.

He dropped out of the novitiate, worked for a travel agency for six months, and began again the following year as a seminarian at Cathedral College in Brooklyn and a candidate for ordination. Now he was on the right track. By the time he had finished the four college years at Cathedral College and Immaculate Conception Seminary, it was clear to his teachers not only that Jerry Gallagher would make a good priest but that he had exceptional gifts. They selected him to go to Rome and study at the Gregorian University.

Those, too, were happy years, although they got off to a slow start. An enormous lecture hall seating five hundred students in serried ranks listening to lecturers holding forth in Latin with accents as various as their homelands is probably not the ideal environment for learning. At first, like most of the other new students, Jerry Gallagher despaired of understanding anything. "I felt stupid," he recalls. But gradually his ear became attuned and the logic of the massive structure of western theology began to emerge. The young man from Long Island with the shining goal of priesthood held out before him hardly noticed the years go by. Almost before he knew it, he found himself lying prostrate on the floor of St. Peter's Basilica waiting for the hands to be placed on his head that would make him a priest forever and open the door to a rich and rewarding life of service.

Graduates of the Gregorian University have traditionally formed a select group from which the future leaders of the church, its bishops and theologians, would be drawn. Perhaps that was the reason the courses were purely academic. There was nothing in the curriculum about pastoral ministry or preaching, nothing to help the students apply what they had learned to the practical work of a parish. Nonetheless, for most of the newly ordained priests, graduation meant returning to their home dioceses to serve as the junior member of the team in a large congregation. If they were to be bishops, they must begin at the bottom of the ladder. Meanwhile, they would learn priesthood by the example of the older priests on the staff and from the orders of the senior pastor. They would pick it up as they went along. So Jerry Gallagher came to the Church of St. Jerome in Flatbush to learn what priesthood meant in a typical New York City parish under the tutelage of a priest of an older generation with very different assumptions about authority.

For Jerry Gallagher, the practical consequence of his questioning of this authority was exile. South Ozone Park was the ecclesiastical equivalent of Siberia, set in a neighborhood plagued by drugs and vandalism. He remembers arriving there for the first time to find three garbage trucks (Department of Sanitation, City of New York) parked outside the church, and he thought to himself, "This really is the end of the line!" The trucks were a daily feature of life at St. Clement Pope; it was where the drivers took their lunch break.

But still there were people in need of ministry and a dedicated corps of lay people worked hard with the clergy to maintain the church as a beacon of hope. Because the authorities were largely indifferent to what happened there, it was a parish with a degree of freedom to experiment and minister in new ways. Rome had decreed that the liturgy should be reshaped; that altars should be freestanding; that the liturgy should be an authentic celebration involving the congregation. And now Fr. Gallagher found himself with colleagues eager to respond to that directive. So the clergy and parish council redesigned the church with the altar as near to the center as possible and hangings over the altar to give it an African feel. They instituted a folk mass with guitars and drums. They used liturgical dance. And worship, as it was meant to do, began to express the life and joy of the community.

The fact that St. Clement Pope was a smaller parish also meant that there was less pressure of parish business and more opportunity to be involved in the community around the church. Before long Fr. Gallagher was the only white member of a board working to help the people of the community through a variety of social programs. For Jerry Gallagher, the bottom line is always people. "I just enjoy people; I love people; I feel for people." And since there were plenty of people in South Ozone Park who needed to be loved, Fr. Gallagher could be happy—up to a point.

But whether in central Brooklyn or farthest Queens, as time went on Jerry Gallagher was increasingly aware of the great gulf between the life of a priest and the life of ordinary people. That gulf was a burden that increasingly took the joy out of ministry. He could not be the kind of priest he wanted to be. He could not really share the lives of men and women and children who, whatever their difficulties, knew an intimacy that Fr. Gallagher was not allowed to know. The separation between his life and theirs seemed ever more unnatural to him. He felt as if he lived somehow on a mountain top and everyone else was down below. However much he might love the priesthood, he had begun to realize that he did not love celibacy. He wanted and needed to share life with someone else. The tension grew steadily and finally he took a four-month leave of absence to allow himself time to think through his vocation again. By the end of that time, he knew he could not go back. His letter telling the pope of his decision continued:

> And yet, I write to you today requesting laicization. This letter is the expression of a long period of prayer and soul-searching. It is written after being on a leave of absence for four

months and after receiving the advice and counsel of good and dedicated priests. My request comes, not out of any discouragement with the priestly ministry, as I am a happy priest, but because I believe my own path to grow in love (and so to be able to serve others more deeply) requires the support and discipline of married love. This decision is not made lightly. The fine priests I have served with these past few years can bear witness that I have thought and prayed and suffered over this decision.

This decision is a personal one and does not reflect any disparagement on the gift of celibacy. It is a beautiful one when combined with a true spirit of poverty—when people can see that the love of Christ is so overwhelming that the riches of this life are relativized. All I can say is that, with my self-knowledge, I now believe that my path to growth includes marriage.

Unfortunately, this was not the letter Fr. Gallagher was supposed to write—and he knew it. He was supposed to write a letter explaining to the pope that he now realized that he was unable to function as a priest because he was psychologically impaired. He was supposed to say that he had become a priest only because his mother wanted it for him and that he now realized his error and asked to be released from his ministry. The trouble was that such a letter would not be true. Jerry Gallagher was a priest because he felt called to be a priest and loved being a priest, and he felt an obligation to tell the pope the truth.

He did not, however, feel obligated to tell the pope the whole truth. Had he done so, Jerry Gallagher might have gone on to say that he had, as a matter of fact, already met a woman with whom he had fallen in love and whom he intended to marry. He had not only left the parish ministry with the idea of getting married; he had even made a short list of young women of his acquaintance whom he thought he might like to date once he was free to do so. One of them, Joyce Ann Kane, known as Joy, had been a nun and a friend of his sister. She had also been having trouble with her vocation and Jerry's sister had sent her to him for counsel. She outlined to him the deadening effect that life in the convent was having on her and sat back to wait for the good father's advice on how to adjust her life to the convent's requirements. "Why don't you stay," he said, "and at your funeral mass they can say, 'She died at twenty-four and was buried at eighty-two?'" Given that way of looking at things, Joy had left her order and gone to work as a lay teacher in a parochial school in Valley Stream.

Valley Stream is on the western border of suburban Nassau County and not far from Jerry Gallagher's parish in South Ozone Park or from the home in central Queens he returned to when he left the parish. So it was not difficult for the priest on leave of absence and the former nun to meet. It didn't take long for Jerry to realize that his list was too long, that Joy was the one he had hoped to meet and with whom he could hope to build a new life. This realization only brought a further dilemma. How could he live with a church that left its members only the choice between obedience and families of limitless size on the one hand, and hypocrisy—disobeying the church's teaching and lying in confession—on the other? But how could he leave the priesthood and marry Joy, knowing it would cost her her job? A teacher in the parochial school might live with a man without marriage and that would cause no problems, but should she marry a former priest, she would be fired.

Deciding that honesty was the best policy, Jerry and Joy agreed that it was better to marry. Jerry would write an honest letter to the pope and they would hope for the best. Three weeks before the date they had chosen for a wedding, the pope's response arrived. Summarized briefly the answer was, "No." Now what? In the Roman Catholic Church all roads may lead to Rome but in South Ozone Park the planes that came over the church were all heading into JFK and there were three chapels at the airport: Roman Catholic, Protestant, and Jewish. Perhaps Joy and Jerry could follow that same flight path and find a Protestant chaplain who would rescue them.

The Protestant chaplain, as it turned out, was the Rev. Marlin Bowman, a priest of the Episcopal Church. Fr. Bowman was very willing to help and, as it turned out, he and Fr. Gallagher spoke the same language of priesthood and sacraments and liturgy—

the language of the Catholic Church. Marlin Bowman and Jerry Gallagher understood each other. The wedding took place in the Protestant chapel at JFK but it was hardly a Protestant wedding. Fr. Bowman presided over the exchange of marriage vows according to the *Book of Common Prayer* and then concelebrated a Roman Catholic nuptial mass with four priests who were friends of the groom. Such a service was probably highly irregular from the standpoint of either church, but it was an accurate expression of where Jerry and Joy Gallagher were in their pilgrimage.

For several years they continued to live in tension between two traditions. Jerry was drawn to a church in which he could be married and exercise his priesthood; Joy had no desire to leave the familiar church for something alien and unknown. And with a new career and new family to consider, there was no time to resolve the matter. One child was born before the year was over and two more in the next three years. A couple of civil service exams led to the offer of a job for Jerry as a probation officer at the Queens County Supreme Court. So, like many other young couples, they set aside the potential sources of conflict and trusted that somehow all would be well. Often that is a recipe for trouble—but sometimes, providentially, it succeeds. As it turned out, this was one of those times.

How does a priest become a probation officer? "I spent," says Jerry, "the most painful two weeks of my life" sitting and listening to the senior probation officer tell war stories: "Then there was the day when...." Jerry fought to stay awake and seem attentive and respectful. Then, suddenly, he was on his own with a caseload of over one hundred individuals not deemed enough of a threat to society to be put behind bars, but not altogether trustworthy citizens either. It was Jerry Gallagher's job to keep in touch with them, to keep society safe from them, and, if possible, to help them work their way back into the good graces of the world around them. He found that he liked the work; it was dealing with people and that made it good. And the team of people he had to work with was good as well. When a call came to consider a job in Dutchess County, he was inclined to turn it down.

There were, in fact, two different openings in Dutchess County for a corrections officer: one at Sing Sing Prison in Ossining, and one at Greenhaven Correctional Institute. Jerry Gallagher followed the parkways north from New York City and came over a rise in the road to see the woods and fields of Dutchess County spread out before him. "Dear God," he remembers thinking, "this is so beautiful." City dwellers in those days moved to Dutchess County for one of two reasons: either they had made such a mess of their lives that they were remanded to Greenhaven or Sing Sing or they had succeeded so well that they had bought an estate and settled down as gentleman farmers. It is a highly desirable place to live—if you have a choice.

Jerry Gallagher had a choice. The apartment in Queens, familiar territory though it was for city people like the Gallaghers, could not compete with the beauty of the country. They found "Joy's dream home" in LaGrangeville, a rural community so small you can seldom find it on the maps, and Jerry learned a new line of work as a corrections counselor at Greenhaven.

"A corrections counselor is a gofer," Jerry explains. "It is crisis intervention. You carry messages for the prisoners—the one who's been threatened by other inmates and needs protection; the one whose wife or girlfriend says she's leaving; the one with health problems who isn't getting the attention he needs. I liked being a probation officer better—I wasn't in prison! I was out on the streets. And it was much more hopeful: the people weren't in prison and so they had a chance to do something with their lives."

But being a corrections counselor, for all its limitations, wasn't uninteresting work. Six months of it led to a position as psychologist. Psychologist? Doesn't that take years of training? "OJT," says Jerry Gallagher with a grin. "On-the-Job Training. I dealt exclusively with murderers and rapists, trying to help them to understand why they did what they did. Group sessions were especially useful; you might con the counselor, but you couldn't con the other inmates. They would make each other face the truth about themselves."

But Jerry Gallagher still hadn't dealt with the truth about himself: the fact that he was a priest. For awhile he and Joy went to a nearby Roman Catholic church and took what part they could in parish life. Jerry even taught an adult course in the New Testament. He and Joy went to communion and had two children baptized in the parish. But the vocation to priesthood was still alive; however fulfilling family life and work might be, Jerry knew there was something missing. Gradually Joy came to see it too and become comfortable with the knowledge that she had married a priest who had to be able to live out that calling. She would not stand in the way.

Jerry also knew that there was a way to be the kind of priest he felt called to be. Another chaplain serving at Greenhaven told him there was an Episcopal priest in Beacon who would help him. And so the Gallaghers found a new parish home at St. Luke's Church and a sponsor in the Rev. Jon Lindenauer.

Is life ever simple? If it were, Jerry Gallagher would have gone to a diocesan conference on ministry and been recommended to the bishop. In the real world, however, everyone at the conference he attended was preoccupied with the oversupply of candidates for ordination and the conviction that the Episcopal Church had too many priests already. Candidates were rejected in batches and Jerry Gallagher, too, was turned down. The commission told him they thought he should spend more time studying Anglican theology. "Anglican theology?" said his friend the chaplain. "There is no such thing as Anglican theology. There's Anglican history and Anglican liturgics, but our theology is simply Catholic theology." But the bishop sent him a reading list and he was invited by Canon William Johnson, an Episcopal theologian who directed a program of studies at the Cathedral of St. John the Divine, to teach a course on the New Testament for the Cathedral Institute of Theology—more on-the-job training.

Needed or not, the delay may have helped make Jerry Gallagher as articulate as he is about the Anglican approach to theology, which he likes to summarize as an inductive rather than a deductive model. The Church of Rome, as he sees it, uses a deductive model: God has acted to lay down certain principles once for all, and our job is to apply them to each new situation. Jerry Gallagher clearly thinks such a model is wrong. "A deductive model limits God. It's idolatry. We take our model and say to God, 'You have to do it this way.' *Potuit, decuit, fecit:* God could, it was fitting, so God did. That canonizes history without a scriptural basis; it says that the way history unfolded was necessarily the will of God. So, for example, the Roman Church would say that Jesus made Peter the first pope and only the Roman Catholic Church has accepted it, therefore only the Roman Catholic Church is the true church. But Jesus wasn't in the business of founding institutions or giving God's singular blessing to a monarchical model of ministry. God's work is always more wonderful than our human models and structures. It's a mistake to take them too seriously. We need to do our thinking inductively, as God does, and bring out what's best in the culture. I love the way the Anglican Church takes human history seriously."

A year later the conference on ministry was ready to take seriously what God had been doing in Jerry Gallagher's history and happily recommended him to the bishop. He was received as a priest of the Episcopal Church in May of 1980. It took him eight years, but finally he was where he wanted to be—or almost.

Though the priesthood Jerry Gallagher had dreamed of was not a part-time ministry, part-time assignments were all that were available for many months. The archdeacon (the administrative assistant to the bishop in a particular region of the diocese) was glad to have another priest available to fill in here and there on Sundays. There was even a four-month stint assisting part-time in one parish, but that wasn't what Jerry Gallagher was waiting for. Almost another year went by, and then the archdeacon called again. Would Jerry be willing to serve as priest-in-charge of a church so small they were thinking of closing it? Of course he would; it was an opportunity to give more time to priesthood and that was all he wanted.

Holy Trinity Church, Pawling, was a parish without much hope; on his first Sunday there, Jerry's wife and family made up forty percent of the congregation. But that was fine. Here was an opportunity to be a priest on a fuller basis. It was one step closer to the dream. Of course, there was still the work to do as a counselor at Greenhaven prison, but he had time to do what needed to be done. "They need to be loved," was his analysis, and that was his idea of priesthood. The congregation responded and grew.

Four years later the archdeacon called again. Could he suggest Fr. Gallagher's name to a parish looking for a priest who would bring them together and help them grow? The parish was in the village of Rhinebeck, a rural Hudson River community so small it doesn't even have a shopping mall. A mixed population of small business owners, blue-collar workers, teachers, technical people from IBM, and weekenders from New York City brought the total population of the village to some twenty-five hundred, with another four or five thousand in the surrounding area. It wasn't Queens, but Joy and Jerry were now established country folk who had found that they liked the small town life.

But the chance to fulfill the dream was still not easy. Married priests can't simply drop everything and go when a call comes. There is a family to think of, a spouse who may have a separate career and other interests, and probably children who have become attached to a school, a neighborhood, and friends. Priests in the Episcopal Church experience the same complexities as other people when opportunities come; in fact, it may be even more complicated for priests. To move to Rhinebeck, for one thing, meant living in the rectory beside the church instead of in Joy's dream house in LaGrangeville. Even apart from all that, it meant giving up a parish Jerry had come to love. It's a measure of his priorities that he found it harder to leave the parish in Pawling than to leave the Roman Catholic Church. So the shining opportunity was balanced by a load of guilt, but the chance to be a priest once again on a full-time basis could not be turned down.

Filled with doubts they made the move, and from the very first day it was all right. The rectory, a four-bedroom colonial, was a little too close to the main route through town for the children to ride their bikes in safety, but the Gallaghers were happy in it until they could find their own house a short distance away. More important, they and the parish were happy with each other and have continued to be.

What has happened in the ten years since? Jerry Gallagher's response is not surprising: "There's been a growing sense of being a real parish family—preaching about it, living it. There were lots of good people here to begin with, some real saints." Although he has brought changes to the parish—an emphasis on outreach to the homeless and homebound elderly, helping the congregation adjust to the new Prayer Book—it is the new spirit of warmth and love in the parish that really matters, Fr. Gallagher will tell you: "It's a sense of joy and thanksgiving about being together. It's an image that we try to project of being God's family, a parish family. We try to be the catalyst to help people's gifts unfold and express our delight when we see it happen. But there's no magic about it, it's just a slow growth in faith."

It seems that Jerry Gallagher is free at last to be the kind of priest God meant him to be, that he has finally come home. There's another kind of evidence as well. The Episcopal Church, like most other churches these days, maintains a central data bank with information on all its clergy. When a parish wants a priest they fill in a form analyzing their special needs and send it in. Computers whir and a list of possibly appropriate priests is generated in response. Most clergy update their "profiles" regularly; who knows what great parish, cathedral, or diocese might need someone just like them? Such a place, however, will not find Jerry Gallagher listed; he has never bothered to fill out the forms. He is where he wants to be and he has no dream beyond being the parish priest in Rhinebeck. "I just want to be a servant in the kingdom," he says. "I've been blessed a thousandfold."

The letter he wrote to the pope years ago ended with a vision: "That one day the Roman Catholic Church will accept a married as well as a celibate clergy, and in that hope I offer my service if that should happen in my lifetime." Is the offer still open? Jerry Gallagher smiles. "I don't feel I've left the priesthood, so I don't have to come back to it. My hope now is that there would be a joyful reunion of two sister communions and we could all serve God together." But so far, there has been no response.

Like Jerry Gallagher, John Mulryan grew up in a world where the church was the center of life, but not one in which its authority was completely unquestioned. The mixed strands of obedience and rebellion that run through his story can be traced back at least to his parents, John and Bridget, who grew up in the same small town in Ireland. The little village of Tuam held no opportunity for young people with ambition, so they came to America in the 1920s, settled in the Bronx, and married. John found work as a freight handler for the Delaware, Lackawanna, and Western Railroad, commuting by subway and ferry to the railroad yards in Hoboken and working steadily at one job all his life, arriving on time and doing the work assigned to him.

John Mulryan, Sr., had grown up in an Ireland ruled by foreigners, the English, and he had a deeply ingrained awareness of the injustice of oppression of any kind. In America there were no English to fight, but there were unjust bosses and an unresponsive government and therefore there was still a need for revolution. John was an admirer of Michael Quill, the fiery, left-wing agitator who led the subway motorman's union. There were others in the labor unions and even the church who carried on the tradition of Irish rebellion against oppressors and overlords. John Mulryan, Sr., did his job and supported his family and church but he also nursed dreams of revolution and a new order. Into that home, in the turmoil of the Depression and the advent of World War II, John Mulryan, Jr., was born.

The Mulryans lived in what was then an Irish neighborhood in the South Bronx. Nearby was St. Ann's, an Episcopal church that was once a bastion of the established order and the church of Gouveneur Morris, one of the signers of the Declaration of Independence. The church stood behind a high fence with a wrought iron gate that was opened on Sundays for the few remaining Episcopalians in the neighborhood. As in Tuam, where a handful of Anglicans worshiped in a twelfth-century cathedral while the rest of the village went to a nineteenth-century Roman Catholic church, most of the community were Roman Catholics.

Young John Mulryan went with his family to St. Luke's Church, where he attended parochial school and learned to serve at the altar. Fr. John P. Sullivan noticed the bright and willing boy and drew him closer. When John reached junior high school, the pastor, Monsignor Mulcahey, gave him duties in the rectory. He would go there after school and sit at the desk doing his homework. When the doorbell rang, John would answer it and say, "Sit here while I call the Father." Before long, John was thinking in terms of vocation.

His first ambition, like Jerry Gallagher's, was to be a teacher, one of the Sacred Heart brothers who taught in the parochial school. The brothers were strong and tough; the paddle was their means of discipline, but they also conveyed a sense of deep commitment to their work. To join the brothers, however, he would have had to go to school in New Jersey and his parents said that was too far away. A better alternative was Cathedral College, which, despite its name, offered four years of high school and two years of college leading on to the diocesan seminary in Dunwoodie. There, in a gold-domed building set high on a commanding hilltop in Yonkers, students were offered the last two years of college and the four years of theology that led to ordination as a priest in the Archdiocese of New York.

Cathedral College was for students setting out on the path toward priesthood—and therefore the program was carefully designed to separate the young men in its care from the corrupting influences of the world. As in other schools, classes were held five days a week, but at Cathedral College the two free days were Sunday and Thursday: Saturday was not a free day because other schools were out then and it was better not to have time to be with other young people if you were studying to be a priest. Yet even here, where carefully selected priests taught the future leaders of the church, the twin Irish traditions of obedience and rebellion were present. It was the McCarthy era, and one history teacher supported the Wisconsin senator's rabid attack on Communism while another, very radical in his politics, seemed to illustrate the senator's theory that communists were everywhere.

John did well at the school. He was president of his class and he won a state scholarship that helped pay for his college years. Dunwoodie in those days was crowded to capacity and beyond with young men like John following a carefully designed path. But two years after reaching Dunwoodie, he was told that he would be going to Rome to complete his education. From a class of sixty, two were selected each year for the honor and opportunity of living at the North American College in Rome itself and attending the Gregorian University to be educated by the greatest scholars in the Roman Catholic world. John, like Jerry Gallagher a few years later, would be among them.

What a time it was to be in Rome! John Mulryan arrived in September of 1958, only weeks after the death of Pope Pius XII. Elected to office at the end of the Great Depression, Pius had been pope for nearly twenty years, leading the church through the Second World War and the worst years of the Cold War. It seemed to John and his classmates that Pius had always been pope. But now he was dead and a new pope must be chosen. Solemnly the cardinals of the Church of Rome arrived to choose the next Vicar of Christ. John Mulryan, still learning his way around the Vatican City, found his way with many others to the great square outside the walls of St. Peter's basilica within which the cardinals were meeting. He stood there in a crowd of hundreds of thousands watching for the smoke signals that would tell them a choice had been made that would shape the future of the church.

At last, after many ballots and plumes of black smoke, the white smoke of election went up and the great crowd cheered as the new pope came out to bless them for the first time. But who had ever heard of Angelo Roncalli? Seventy-seven years old at his election, the new Pope John XXIII had served the church well, climbing slowly through the bureaucracy by a readiness to follow orders and carry out, without complaint, the wishes of those above him. It seemed to many as if the cardinals had concluded that no one could replace the autocratic Pius, and so they had elected no one, an amiable and noncontroversial man who would hold the office for a few years until some new and better leader emerged. After all, Pope Pius had set the church on a firm path and there was no real need for dramatic change.

Three months later, the new pope stunned the world by announcing his intention to summon an ecumenical council, the first in almost a century, and to begin the work of *aggiornomento*, the modernization and renewal of the church for the mission of a new age.

As a result, the four years of John Mulryan's theological studies were a time of intensive preparation for the council and rising expectations. The new pope was a warm and caring man who visited prisoners and reached out to children. Perhaps the church could be molded in an image more like that. Meanwhile, however, life went on much as it had always done. John and his classmates, immersed in the study of history and theology, had little time to consider the future of the church or its relationship to the world.

For a student today, the thought of Rome conjures up visions of romance and adventure—coffee houses and trattoria, Anna Magnani on a motor scooter and the Coliseum at midnight—but for the students at the Gregorian Institute it meant daily excursions *(cammerati)* to one of the ancient churches of Rome in groups of eight accompanied by a senior student, called a beadle. Blue cassocks with a red sash and white collar marked them as seminarians. John remembers an old woman hissing *"Bagarocchi!"* ("cockroaches") as they passed by. Students could save their *lira* and go out occasionally to eat in an Italian restaurant or even assuage their nostalgia for America with a hamburger at the Madison House. Once a year, the students were given a month's vacation, traveling through Europe in groups to avoid temptation and staying in student hostels and the cheapest hotels they could find. In France, John remembers being followed down the stairs by a large rat as they were leaving their hotel.

Dramatic moments tended to be ecclesiastical. John was there for the crowning of the new pope and remembers how, as the pope went down the aisle of St. Peter's, a monk who had been assigned the part said to him, "Remember that you are dust, and to dust you shall return." But even in the sacred and timeless precincts of the Vatican, the shifting politics of the outer world intruded from time to time. President Eisenhower came to visit the pope, the first American president to do so. Three helicopters dropped down on the sports field where the seminarians played baseball and football, and kept their rotors turning—and the students on the sidelines—while the president went by limousine to the papal apartments.

Year by year the students advanced through the minor orders—porter, lector, exorcist, acolyte, subdeacon—and then, in September of their senior year, they were made deacons. In December, in the great basilica of St. Peter, they were ordained at last to the priesthood. In the summer of 1962, John returned to New York as a priest to begin the work for which he had been so carefully prepared.

He was assigned to the staff of the Church of St. Rose of Lima on Washington Heights, a Manhattan neighborhood centered on the great Columbia-Presbyterian Hospital and Delafield City Hospital, but filled with all the variety of life for which the city is known. There were three assistant pastors and a hospital chaplain. They took turns answering the phone at night and responding to emergencies of every sort. One night someone was hit by a subway train, and a policeman searched for some recognizable piece of the head to bring to Fr. Mulryan for anointing. He was deeply moved by the quiet care with which the police sought to enable his ministry. Another night he was called at 3 a.m. to anoint a body already cold and in the morgue. Fr. Mulryan had been given careful instruction on how he should not anoint a body from which life had long departed, but he remembers thinking, "What harm can it do? The family will be comforted, so why not?" Theology and the world came together and the rigid outlines of a logical system had to be modified to meet human need.

Priesthood was a joy. Fr. Mulryan was an accepted part of a thoroughly human neighborhood and shared its laughter as well as its grief. Two years went by in a moment and the diocese summoned John for a conference. "We want you to study," they said. "Study what?" asked John. "What would you like to study?" they replied. Somewhere it had been noted that the young priest in Washington Heights had academic aptitude and should be encouraged, but no protocols seemed to be in place and John was left to define his future for himself. Columbia was an obvious place to go and English literature had an appeal. John took himself to Columbia and was told he had no background for studies in English but would be nicely fitted to the department of medieval history. He began to study medieval history. An apartment was found at Iona College in the suburbs. Fr. Mulryan would commute to Columbia to pursue his studies and sharpen his intellectual skills while serving as a part-time chaplain to the students at Iona and saying a daily mass.

The middle sixties were years of turmoil at Columbia. Students rose in rebellion over the Vietnam war and closed the college down. Detesting the war but letting obedience outweigh rebelliousness, John met with professors in their apartments and tried to get on with his work as best he could. But the chaos of the time inevitably left its mark. Life went on, but the familiar guidelines could no longer be relied on; everything, it seemed, was open to question and change.

Two years later, the diocese called again and said, "We need you to go to Poughkeepsie to teach in the high school there." So John went to Poughkeepsie, sixty miles up the Hudson River. The new post was a diocesan high school, Our Lady of Lourdes, but it was not like Cathedral College when John had studied there. Now the students carried guitars and listened to the Beatles; their parents were second- and third-generation Americans who had begun to move up the social ladder. It was no longer a matter of pride when a daughter decided to be a nun or a son felt called to priesthood. Now the response might well be to send them to a psychiatrist.

John Mulryan also was looking for some further meaning in his vocation. He was reading books by Teilhard de Chardin, a Jesuit and paleontologist who had searched for dinosaur bones in the Gobi desert. Teilhard had written about an earth that was evolving toward an "Omega point" where all would be fulfilled in love. His imaginative theology did not fit the traditional categories and so he had been silenced by the Vatican. Nonetheless, he had continued to develop his ideas in books and essays that stirred a wide response when they were finally published after his death in 1955. He was buried in an inconspicuous grave at St. Andrew's, a Jesuit novitiate on the Hudson River not far from Poughkeepsie.

John went one day to find the grave—and kneeling there beside the grave was Timothy Leary, one of the best known prophets of the sixties, who proclaimed a world of free love and mind-expanding drugs. John recognized him from the pictures in the newspapers and asked why he was there. "I'm here out of respect for Teilhard de Chardin," said Leary. "So am I," said John. But what sign could have marked more clearly the rightness of the Vatican's suspicions of the dangers inherent in Teilhard's thoughts than the homage of Timothy Leary? And what would the authorities have said had they seen their promising young priest communing with the spirit of Teilhard de Chardin and talking with Timothy Leary?

In the spring John was informed of yet another move, this time to Cardinal Spellman High School in the northeast Bronx as chairman of the social studies department. But John was not pleased. "Is there someone somewhere," he wondered, "who knows what I can do and is moving me around in a coherent plan, or am I simply being used to fill holes and keep the ship afloat?" Every time he had begun to get his bearings—in parish life, in a doctoral program, in a new parish—he had been reassigned. John thought of himself as an obedient sort of person—"but when an obedient person gets pushed to the wall," he says now, "obedience turns into anger." John Mulryan was becoming angry.

His anger found a focus in July of 1968. A commission had been formed to study the subject of birth control and prepare a report for the pope's guidance. The committee had drawn its report with care and recommended that papal resistance to birth control be abandoned. The new pope, Paul VI, had been steering a careful course between the high hopes raised by John XXIII and a deeply entrenched conservative resistance, but there was great hope in the church of an opening here, at the place where theology touched people's lives most intimately. The pope studied his commission's report—and overruled it. Sexual relationships must always be open to the procreation of life; artificial means of birth control were prohibited.

The papal encyclical, *Humanae Vitae*, was a turning point for the Roman Church perhaps more critical than Vatican II, for here the church had taken a stand that many of its members found themselves unable to accept. Confidence in the unchanging authority of the church had been shaken by the reforms of Vatican II, but at least those reforms brought hope of a more humane and responsive church. Now those hopes were gone, but the church's authority was no longer beyond all question. If the Latin mass could vanish overnight, nothing was fixed and certain anymore, and certainly not a papal encyclical that ran counter to the practical common sense of its members. They would, for the most part, remain loyal to the church, but they would never again respond to its teachings without questioning. They would select the doctrines they could accept and those they would reject. Priests, too, would learn to be silent or to reinterpret. But that was not a comfortable path for John Mulryan: "As a Roman Catholic, I wasn't very tolerant of ambiguity."

Torn between the ministry he loved and a church unable to turn a human face toward people's needs, John saw no future for himself in the church. He liked the work of a parish: meeting, helping, counseling people, taking part in the liturgy. "It was fun," he says, "and it still is." But there was no way, in conscience, to be a priest in a church that seemed to have no concern for people. "The church seemed to be going down a path that was destructive, not supportive. There was a sense that a door had closed." But another door was opening.

The telephone rang one evening in Fr. Mulryan's apartment. A priest he knew had a friend looking for an apartment. Apartments in Manhattan are hard to find, but death does make some available and one accepted method of apartment hunting is to call the local priest and ask who has been buried lately. John knew of no apartments himself but he called the local undertaker, who did. When John called his friend back with the name of the real estate agent, a woman answered the phone.

The conversation that followed lasted for eight hours. Jan Kalna had grown up in the same church and society on the verge of change as John had, but as a lay person she was able to work for change without concern for the rules and regulations that controlled the life of a priest. While John, in the midst of turmoil, had managed to go on with his studies at Columbia, Jan had interrupted her college career to work on voter registration campaigns in Louisiana. Daniel Berrigan, a Jesuit deeply involved in the anti-war movement, had stayed in her home and she had gone to the airport with others to welcome home from Guatemala two Maryknoll missionaries who had been expelled from the country because of their work in that corrupt and war-torn society. Their common background and common concerns—contrasted with their very different positions—gave them much to talk about. Jan sensed that John was lonely, that he was looking for someone to confide in, someone to whom he could talk honestly and openly about his life. They met the next day and went for a ride down Riverside Drive. They met again the next day and drove further. They drove around in Brooklyn and New Jersey, outside the Archdiocese of New York as much as possible so as not to be seen together. They became engaged.

The Archdiocese, unaware of the changes taking place in Fr. Mulryan's life, called once more, this time with an offer he would have been eager for at one time: Roman Catholic chaplain at Columbia University. But now John had other plans and he decided the church could no longer use him to fill its vacancies. He drew up a resume and sent it out to a number of schools in the area. A high school in Manhasset, a pleasant suburb on the north shore of Long Island, responded and offered John a position teaching history and social studies. He accepted it and settled down to finish out his term at Cardinal Spellman.

John and Jan were married in the summer of 1970 by a justice of the peace. She had wanted a church wedding but he was too angry at the church—not only at the Roman Catholic Church but at all churches, without distinction. Like many other Roman Catholics, he knew only one church; if it had failed, there were no alternatives. Some priests in that situation, like Jerry Gallagher, write to the pope for permission to be laicized and married. "Why should I do that?" asked John. "Why should I write to ask permission for a normal human activity? That would be to admit that what I was doing was wrong—and it was not wrong."

Happily married but without any savings, he and Jan scraped together a few pieces of furniture and managed to survive the summer on Jan's small salary as an elementary school teacher in a parochial school until John's first paycheck came in. John had always liked teaching and the new environment was stimulating and challenging; thoughts of church and priesthood were pushed aside by the excitement of a new beginning. Then one day Jan went for a routine eye examination and the doctor saw something that concerned him. He suggested Jan go to St. Luke's Hospital to see a specialist. The diagnosis was melanoma, with the prognosis very uncertain. Surgery and chemotherapy followed.

Stumbling back into the street at the end of a chemotherapy session, John noticed through his tears a Gothic building with a cross and an open door. John had been away from the church, any church, for several years but in this crisis his alienation no longer mattered. He made his way into the vast, dark space of the Cathedral of St. John the Divine and collapsed into the first seat he found. That was where a canon of the cathedral found him.

Canon Edward N. West was a legend in his own time. For twenty years he had served on the staff of the Cathedral of St. John the Divine, the largest Gothic structure in the world, as Canon Sacrist, director of ceremonies. When Canon West raised his finger prelates processed, acolytes acted, and thunderous chords came crashing down from the organ loft. In his later years, he affected a style of dress that only enhanced the legend. With a full gray beard, headgear copied out of a medieval manuscript, chains and crosses hanging from his neck, and a staff in one hand, he looked like a Christian Moses about to cross the Red Sea or a monk who had stumbled out of an isolated Russian monastery into the streets of uptown Manhattan. Those who penetrated to his office or apartment found it cluttered with icons and obscure liturgical objects; one had the feeling of being in a museum or on the stage set for a Gothic thriller.

But behind this façade was a deeply caring pastor. It was also said of Canon West that he knew every gardener and maintenance man on the cathedral staff—their families, their illnesses, their children's troubles with school. He was said to be the only member of the cathedral staff who spoke to them all, so it was not surprising that he noticed one day a young man sitting in a back row of the cathedral and weeping. Canon West sat down beside him and said, "Tell me all."

John Mulryan told him all. "It just came pouring out," he remembers: five years of frustration and pain and, at the end of it all, a wife in St. Luke's Hospital across the street from the cathedral with a diagnosis of melanoma. The canon listened, and finally he said, "Come back and worship with us on Sunday." John came with Jan when she could leave the hospital, and there in the great cathedral John found the church and the community he had always hoped to find.

Meanwhile Jan's treatment went well and she was sent home—though chemotherapy would continue for a year and regular checkups are now a permanent part of her life. Each Sunday she and John made a pilgrimage to the cathedral and there, in the vast, echoing Gothic space, they discovered together a pattern of worship and a community both deeply familiar and wildly different. There was, first of all, the liturgy: for the most part it was very familiar and done with a deep reverence. But even in the liturgy there were discoveries, including an assistant who could swing two pots of incense simultaneously in great circles, one with each hand—something John had never seen before. He watched with the respect one professional pays to another. John also noted that Canon West's sermons were always gender-inclusive, another new experience that impressed him.

St. John's was no ordinary cathedral. Its dean, the Very Rev. James P. Morton, believed that the cathedral should be, as medieval cathedrals had been, a center of community life and a space in which every aspect of the community—even a community as diverse as New York City—could find a place. No one could be neutral about the result. The *National Review* called the cathedral "God's great blimp hanger" and renamed it "St. John the Divine Pantheist." The dean filled the cathedral with animals to celebrate the feast day of St. Francis of Assisi and the unity of creation. "Come unto me all you who travail and are heavy laden," wrote a columnist, "and I will anoint your goldfish." Even a generally positive article in *Newsweek* admitted that "some of Morton's cathedral extravaganzas do violate good sense as well as good taste."

But John Mulryan was ready for a church unhampered by the past and by papal pronouncements, and for him the cathedral was "glorious fun, like a wonderful candy store." One Sunday a clown came down the aisle in the procession and mimed the sermon; on another, Buckminster Fuller was there to expound the theory of geodesic domes. One night they sat in the dark, unheated cathedral to watch a medieval mystery play. The variety was unending, but always there was the ancient and noble liturgy centering and shaping whatever happened. Sometimes the cathedral would be packed as thousands came for a great event, and other days sixty or seventy people would huddle in the corners of the great choir. The small continuing congregation welcomed John and Jan with no questions asked.

"The place was filled with characters," John remembers, and many of them were responding to the dean's interest in environmental issues. One Sunday the coffee hour was riven with controversy when someone noticed that the coffee was being served in styrofoam cups, and the dean was told to renew the face of the earth beginning with paper cups. Controversy also broke out over the cathedral school when the dean summarily fired the headmaster. It was John's first introduction to controversy in the Episcopal Church and what interested him most was that the dismissed headmaster was given the pulpit for a farewell address, along with an opportunity to state his side of the case. He was even given a farewell party. It seemed that here two people could have an honest disagreement and come to a parting of the ways, but the loser was not silenced or condemned to outer darkness. There was room in the church for both.

The Mulryans were invited to join an inquirers' class to prepare to be received into the Episcopal Church. They met in Canon West's study, where the shelves were lined with books and the floor and desk piled high, but the canon knew where every one of them was and would stop in mid-sentence to dash across the room and come back with the exact book he needed to make a point. The class read *The Screwtape Letters* by C. S. Lewis and discussion ranged far and wide. "We didn't learn much about the Episcopal Church that I can remember, but we learned it was open and accepting and tolerated ambiguity"—and John was more accepting of ambiguity than he had been.

Then one Sunday Canon West said, "Why don't you become an Episcopal priest? I'll give you the forms to fill out." Put that way, it sounded simple, but the process once begun turned out to be endlessly complicated. After he filled out the forms, there was a weekend conference for candidates for ordination to meet with a committee of clergy and lay people, to discuss vocation and struggle to articulate a sense of calling. For John and other Roman Catholic priests, the challenge was to express one's familiarity and comfort with the different environment of the Episcopal Church. The commission on ministry liked John enormously but had doubts about his exposure to the Episcopal Church. Was the cathedral in all its uniqueness an adequate introduction to the real world of Anglicanism? John was directed to go to another, more typical parish and see whether he was drawn to the Episcopal Church or only to its eccentric cathedral.

That is how he arrived at Christ Church, Bronxville, a sedate, upper-middle-income community of bankers and lawyers and executives. Christ Church's worship had been molded into a distinctive pattern many years earlier and still used elaborate vestments, a highly stylized liturgy, and an occasional whiff of incense. The Mulryans learned that Bronxville was not the Bronx. Restraint was in order. Clothing, conduct, everything was understated, decorous, tasteful. They learned that the Episcopal variety of Catholicism had five notes, not four: one, holy, catholic, apostolic—and picky. Whether the matter in hand was the menu for a covered dish supper or the details of the liturgy, factions formed and endless debate ensued. There were extraordinary battles over whether or not to serve chipped beef. "Prayer books, hymnals, gender—whatever happens, there's a fight!" But two years as part of the congregation and long sessions with the rector, courses at the General Theological Seminary, and meetings with the suffragan bishop for guidance did provide a wider window on the church. On December 20, 1981, just twenty years to the day after he was ordained to the priesthood in St. Peter's Basilica, he was accepted as a priest of the Episcopal Church in a solemn liturgy at Christ Church, Bronxville.

John Mulryan's path into parish ministry in the Episcopal Church led him to understand that it is not a church in which one waits for assignments from on high. The Mulryans lived in Great Neck, Long Island, and there are three struggling Episcopal churches serving that predominantly Jewish community. Walking one day in the neighborhood, John noticed that the signboard outside St. Paul's Church had no rector's name. He learned that they had had no priest for two years because they couldn't afford one. John thought, "But I have a full-time job. Maybe they *could* afford me!" More inquiries brought about a meeting with the wardens of the parish and then a meeting with the bishop, who was interested in what he called "tent-maker" ministries: priests who, like the tent-making apostle Paul, would earn their own living and carry on a ministry in the church as well. All was arranged almost before the ink was dry on John Mulryan's new certificate of priesthood in the Episcopal Church.

St. Paul's doesn't grow but it holds its own, always somehow drawing enough new members to replace those who die or move away. Here, too, Episcopalians are "one, holy, catholic, apostolic and picky." They have huge and generally cheerful fights over many minor issues, but manage to get on with the task of building a church that worships together in an integrated community. Worship still stands at the center and the little church provides for John Mulryan the home every Christian life needs and the chance to be a priest—a priest free to ask questions and to live with an ambiguity openly recognized and sometimes even celebrated.

For him, the bivocational life still works well. John can wax as eloquent about high school teaching as about *Humanae Vitae* but in a much more positive vein. "High school teaching keeps you young, alive, the blood flowing. Occasionally you see lights go on and it makes you feel you've accomplished something. And teenagers: society generally doesn't like them because they're messy. But I enjoy them. It's fun." John and Jan have an adopted son now, a teenager himself, and a big old rectory has lots of room for his friends to drop by. And what does John teach his students? Ambiguity. "Preaching to kids doesn't work. Issues of faith and morals come up and you have to make sure both sides are presented fairly. You teach the Crusades, the age of Imperialism, the American frontier. There's the serious and messy problem of human beings who do wonderful things for the wrong reason and terrible things with the best intentions. You can't have a moral rule without exceptions or you deny God's freedom." And John Mulryan values God's freedom.

Fifteen years ago, as the Episcopal Church seethed in controversy over a new revision of the prayer book and the ordination of women as priests, the Vatican set up a process for accepting Episcopal priests, even married ones, into the Roman Catholic Church. They would have to be reordained since the Roman Catholic Church does not recognize Anglican orders, but they could serve as priests without any long process of examination and training. Occasionally they could even bring their congregations and (rarely) their church buildings with them. Nonetheless, for all the controversy and special arrangements, fewer than one hundred Episcopal clergy have taken advantage of the opportunity, while some two hundred fifty Roman Catholic priests have, in that same time, been received into the Episcopal Church. Some six hundred former Roman Catholic priests are said to be serving today in the Episcopal Church. The one bishop of the Episcopal Church who recently joined the Roman Catholic Church came back, disillusioned, in less than a year.

The Episcopal Church has no special process for receiving Roman Catholic priests, though it receives many. They are treated very much like any other candidate for ordination: there must be recommendations from a parish and priest, recommendation by a diocesan screening process, and finally approval by the standing committee and diocesan bishop. At that point, when a seminary graduate would be ordained, a former Roman Catholic priest is simply "received" as a priest into the Episcopal

Church. No "reordination" is necessary since the Episcopal Church does recognize Roman Catholic orders, just as it recognizes Roman Catholic confirmations and simply receives lay people who have already been confirmed by a Roman Catholic bishop.

For John Mulryan and Jerry Gallagher, the contrast between the Roman and Anglican understanding of authority has been dramatically evident in their experiences since they became priests in the Episcopal Church. The heavy-handed authority that exiled Jerry Gallagher to South Ozone Park and used John Mulryan to fill vacancies without any clear sense of purpose was replaced by a system that left clergy and people free to work out their own destinies with only minimal guidance from the bishop and bishop's staff. That gift of freedom can also create frustrations, of course, but many who have experienced a system without such freedom are more than willing to pay that price.

The proper balance between authority and freedom is something human beings have been working on for centuries and no church so far can claim to have worked it out perfectly. The great Russian novelist, Fyodor Dostoevsky, in his novel *The Brothers Karamazov* depicts a Grand Inquisitor who, during the Spanish Inquisition, arrests Jesus himself. Freedom, in the Grand Inquisitor's view, is too dangerous a gift for human beings to cope with successfully and Jesus was mistaken in allowing his followers to use it. Freedom, indeed, can be dangerous, but just as parents know they must let their children learn to use freedom responsibly, so, Anglicans feel, the church must encourage its members to accept the responsibility of freedom and use it to enhance human life. The Anglican way can be frustrating to those who want clear directions, but at its best it enables human beings to grow into maturity and take responsibility in creative ways.

Human life, as John Mulryan likes to emphasize, is full of ambiguity. There is often much to be said on both sides of a question. Perhaps that is why Jesus, like modern rabbis, taught so often in parables, not papal bulls. A papal bull gives a clear answer to a specific question but may easily become obsolete as new questions arise. A parable or story, on the other hand, invites us to consider the various aspects of life and remains relevant in many changing circumstances. When Jesus was asked what it means to "love your neighbor," he told the story of the Good Samaritan. When he was asked about forgiveness, he told the story of the Prodigal Son. These stories illuminate our understanding without giving clear directions and they still exert a deep influence on western civilization.

Papal bulls, on the other hand, have spoken to a wide variety of issues over the centuries. They have attempted to give the faithful guidance on such matters as war and peace, economic organization, and issues like birth control, abortion, and the ordination of women. Some of these statements have been useful; others, like *Humanae Vitae*, have caused deep divisions in the church and alienated many. The bishops of the Anglican Communion and the General Convention of the Episcopal Church have also spoken on these issues, but their statements are intended to guide, not control, the debate. Members are free to form different opinions and work with others to attempt to persuade the bishops and leadership of the church. Such differences of opinion are tolerable (though sometimes distressing!) because Anglicans find their unity in worship rather than in statements of faith and principle.

From time to time this approach is so frustrating even to Episcopalians that groups within the church try to force others to agree with them or leave. The difficulty with this approach is that it would create a church in which the primary objective is human agreement. In the first days of the church, when the authorities in Jerusalem wanted to arrest Christians and put them in jail, a wise member of the Jewish Council said it would be better to leave them alone, "because if this plan or this undertaking is of human origin, it will fail; but if it is of God, you will not be able to overthrow them—in that case you may even be found fighting against God!" (Acts 5:38-39). That approach takes patience and a strong faith, but in the long run it gives Christians opportunity to seek the truth in freedom. Episcopalians have usually preferred to live with a good deal of confusion and difference of opinion than to silence those with whom they disagree.

When asked what authority they look to for guidance, Anglicans have usually spoken of scripture, tradition, and reason. Scripture comes first, since it bears witness to what God has done in history and enables us to see who God is as revealed in human lives, especially the life of Jesus Christ. Tradition includes the life of the church and the understandings Christians have come to under the guidance of the Holy Spirit. Anglicans turn especially to the witness of the church of the first centuries and decisions of ecumenical councils before the church became divided. These sources of authority must, in turn, commend themselves to our reason. Episcopalians can be accused of being too rational in an unreasonable world, but God created human reason and presumably expects us to use it. William Laud, Archbishop of Canterbury in the seventeenth century, spoke of the way human beings must use reason to come to grips with scripture and tradition and yet, at the same time, remember that reason alone is never enough, that the mystery of God cannot be contained by human minds.

To use reason, and to respond willingly to authority not because we are compelled to obey but because God's love draws us, we must be free. We might almost say that the Anglican Communion *invites* its members to be "cafeteria Catholics," hoping that they, as mature and intelligent Christians, will choose those items from the menu that will do the most to nourish them. The rich Christian tradition spreads out a feast for us, and our fellow Christians—theologians, bishops, priests, and lay people—will recommend certain items on the menu, even urge us for our own good to take this or that. But finally the decision must be ours and we will be responsible for the consequences, whether they are spiritual starvation, malnutrition, indigestion, or growth into what St. Paul calls "maturity,...the measure of the full stature of Christ" (Eph. 4:13).

6

Controversy and Common Sense

Matthew Fox

"My decision to embrace the Anglican tradition is about including some anglo-saxon (and celtic) *common sense* into twenty-first century catholicism." *(Matthew Fox)*

James A. Pike loved controversy. It is said that when he was rector of Christ Church, Poughkeepsie, and learned that Vassar College had a policy of not letting clergy come on the campus, he called some newspapers and told them that if they would like a story they could come on a certain day and see his eviction from the college grounds. Then he called the college to let them know where and when they would need to be to enforce their policy. The college, less eager for controversy, ignored him, and he proceeded to exercise a ministry on the college grounds.

Christmas 1951 saw the New York City release of *Baby Doll*, a new movie based on a play by Tennessee Williams, perhaps the best-known playwright of the day. The play dealt with sexuality more openly than was customary at that time, and the Roman Catholic Archbishop of New York, Francis Cardinal Spellman—also no stranger to controversy—went into the pulpit of St. Patrick's Cathedral on Sunday morning to warn the souls entrusted to his care that seeing *Baby Doll* would be a sin against the church and against America. The following Sunday James Pike, then dean of the Cathedral of St. John the Divine in New York City, also went into his pulpit to tell the congregation assembled before him that he had seen the movie, and *Baby Doll* was in fact less sensual than Cecil B. Demille's *The Ten Commandments*, which the Cardinal had commended. "Those who do not want the sexual aspect of life included in the portrayal of real-life situations," Pike added, "had better burn their Bibles as well as abstain from the movies."

For the better part of a generation James Pike, as priest, dean, and finally Bishop of California, continued to provoke controversy not only with those outside the Episcopal Church but with those within it as well. Some of his brother bishops at last accused him of heresy, but many other people were drawn to a church that had room within its ranks for a man who thought that challenging and questioning was the best way to grow and that each age needed to find new ways to express the eternal truths of the gospel.

A generation later, the Episcopal Church continues to find room for controversial figures. John Spong, Bishop of Newark, pleases some and raises the hackles of others. Matthew Fox, who has been received as a priest of the Episcopal Church, was silenced by the Vatican for his innovative advocacy of a revitalized spirituality for ordinary Christians. Fox would probably not make a good bishop, even in the Episcopal Church, tolerant though we may be of bishops who question traditions and challenge authority. The load of administrative and pastoral responsibility commonly thrust on bishops would be more likely to stifle than stimulate his creativity.

Fox's parents, his father especially, taught him to respect authority, but strong-minded parents are not likely to produce compliant children. Matthew Fox learned early how to maintain his independence: required to lick his plate clean, he learned to hold the food he didn't like in his cheek until the meal was over and he could spit it out somewhere else. More significant still in molding Fox's character was a critical illness with polio at the age of twelve. Polio epidemics in those days before the Salk vaccine were a frequent summer occurrence, sweeping through communities without warning and leaving some children dead and others paralyzed. One playmate of Fox's had died the summer before and Fox himself came very near death.

He survived, but his legs were paralyzed and no one could promise that he would ever walk again. Kept in the hospital for nearly a year, where even his brothers and sisters could speak to him only through a window, the long isolation changed him profoundly. And not only the isolation—for among those who came to visit was Brother Martin, a Dominican whose quiet and thoughtful manner was in striking contrast to that of Fox's father, a domineering football coach. Timothy Fox (he would become Matthew when he entered religious life) had already apparently made some sort of commitment to serve God if he survived the illness; long conversations with Brother Martin helped give a clearer sense of vocation.

The teenage years, so often a time of rebelliousness and confusion, became for Timothy Fox a time of sharply focused preparation for a life of service. "There was a difference inside me," Fox says of his months of illness. "My polio experience baptized me into a mystical awareness."[1] After that, he went to mass every day, walking four miles to the nearest church when his family went away for the summer and staying afterward for long talks with the priests. He went to a summer camp the Dominican Order operated where young men could sample the life of the community. At nineteen he joined the order.

Novices in the Dominican Order endured a discipline not radically different from boot camp for the Marines. Days of chanting and meditation and plain hard work began every morning at five o'clock. Novices were also cut off from their families; Matthew—as he was now to be called—was not even allowed to attend his sister's wedding. Others might have found it hard, but Fox had learned about isolation and discipline from his year with polio and thrived on it.

What he did not thrive on, however, was unquestioning acceptance. Why do monks chant? Why do they keep times of silence? What is the value of celibacy? No one else seemed to ask these questions, and since no one seemed to have the answers that Matthew Fox needed, he began to explore and to find his own answers. One answer he discovered was that discipline and silence free the nonrational side of the brain and enable the mystical experience which lies at the heart of the religious life. Fox seemed to have a natural aptitude for such experience. He shocked his superiors by asking permission to spend a summer living with a colony of hermits on Victoria Island on the west coast of Canada. Weeks in a candlelit, snake-infested hut were pure joy for him, diminished only by a lingering sense that his vocation was not limited to the mystical life, that there was injustice to be confronted in the world and that he must find a way to bring these two callings together.

Ordination to the priesthood in 1967 was, therefore, not so much a goal achieved as another step toward his real calling: to understand the workings of the Spirit and the ways of human response. He wrote for guidance to Thomas Merton, one of the great spiritual teachers of this century, and at his suggestion went to study in Paris. It was a time of turmoil not only in America but also in France: student protests would paralyze Paris for days at a time. There, where Thomas Aquinas and Meister Eckhart had worked to revolutionize the thought of their day, revolution seemed again to be in the air—and Fox was thrilled to be part of it. He was chosen as spokesman for a group of young Dominicans seeking to revolutionize the order and, except for the timely intervention of friends, would have been ordered home by his outraged superiors. Instead, he completed his studies with a thesis studying American religious life as revealed in the pages of *Time*. In exploring the relationship between religion and popular culture, he had found his life's work.

In the teaching of a senior member of his order, Pere Marie-Dominique Chenu, Fox had also discovered an approach to theology that enabled him to analyze the role of religion in society. Chenu pointed out that there are two main traditions in Christian theology, one focused on the fall and redemption, the other on creation. "Scales fell from my eyes," wrote Fox. "I was bumped from my horse! The most pressing question I had brought with me to Paris: how do mysticism and social justice relate (if at all)?—now had a context! Creation spirituality would bring it all together for me: the scriptural and Jewish spirituality;...science and spirituality; politics and prayer; body and spirit; science and religion; Christianity and other world religions."[2]

The Dominicans, however, were more interested in encouraging Matthew Fox to explore the relationship between his abstract studies and the real world of the institutional church. From the excitement and turmoil of Paris he was dispatched to a teaching post at the Aquinas Institute in Dubuque, Iowa. Dubuque is different from Paris in many ways but, determined though he was to avoid controversy and keep a low profile, Matthew Fox was able to find the seeds of revolution even there. It seemed he could no more avoid raising questions than the tall Iowa corn could stop growing.

Two months into his first term he was asked to preside at the community mass and he decided to preach on the theme of "What Celibacy is Not." As Fox expounded it, celibacy had to do with a sense of wonder and an awakened erotic playfulness. Sexuality was not something to be suppressed in fear but to be appreciated and expressed in many ways. The response among the students was immediate and when an election for vice-prior was held not long after, Fox was the nearly unanimous choice of the students. The faculty, however, was not pleased and the vote was "cassated"—the faculty simply overruled the students. Some students left the order in frustration and Fox himself moved to Chicago and finished out his responsibilities in Dubuque as a commuter.

And now Fox began to develop his own career, still in connection with the order but no longer "on assignment." Increasingly, he would set his own course. He moved to Boston and published his first book, a book on prayer intended to draw the interest of those for whom the established patterns of prayer had no appeal. The title he chose, *On Becoming a Musical, Mystical Bear*, was designed to get attention. The cover design on the paperback edition shows a smiling, light orange bear with filmy wings floating over a bed of flowers like a balloon in the Macy's Thanksgiving Day parade, with flowers in its mouth, a drum suspended from its neck, and drumsticks firmly clutched in its paws. "Spirituality American Style" is the subtitle. Is this serious?

In fact, it is very serious. After the title page comes a quotation from T. S. Eliot that sums up the purpose:

> Perhaps it is not too late...
> And I must borrow every changing shape
> To find expression...dance, dance
> Like a dancing bear.

Matthew Fox was asking, out of his commitment to the spiritual life, whether it is too late to draw a contemporary world into acts of response to its Creator. Perhaps Fox saw himself as a dancing bear who would take on whatever shape was needed to reach out to people indifferent to the spiritual life or unable to respond to what the church was doing. He quotes a business-man who told him, "I know that I still pray like I did when I was a child. Surely there must be such a thing as an adult way of praying." This, says Fox, is the result of "a religion that is geared financially, institutionally, and intellectually to children" and helps to explain "one motive for the exit in a twelve-month period alone last year of fifty percent of American Catholic seminari-ans."[3] *On Becoming a Musical, Mystical Bear* is a book designed to teach adults to pray, but first of all to persuade them that prayer is something they are already instinctively drawn to do. "Prayer," wrote Fox, "is a radical response to life....A response is sponta-neous (from the Latin *sponte*, of one's own will): it is free, it is mine. We respond *because we feel like it*, such as a youth does on diving into the sea fully clothed or a child does on spotting candy or bright lights: it is a simple utterance of one's deep feelings."[4]

The book got people's attention, as it was designed to do, but not only the attention of lay people interested in developing a spiritual life. The National Conference of Directors of Religious Education called on Fox to conduct a study of how spirituality was being taught in America, and Mundelein College in Chicago offered him the opportunity to put his ideas into practice. The result was the Institute in Culture and Creation Spirituality. Now he had a forum in which he could try to develop approaches to spirituality to which contemporary Americans would respond.

But *On Becoming a Musical, Mystical Bear*, aimed though it was at those outside professional theological circles, contained inevitably a challenge to those within. His preface to the paperback edition begins: "In this book I have tried to present the groundwork for a spirituality that is non-repressive and non-ideological. One that frees instead of coerces...." Who did Fox see as opposed to freedom, and coercing instead of setting free? He speaks of "churches bent on preaching a psychologized morality (sex and drink are no-nos) instead of leading a combat with the evil spirits of our times," and he cites Camilo Torres, who said that he "stopped offering Mass to live out the love for my neighbor in the temporal, economic, and social order. When my neighbor no longer has anything against me...then I will offer Mass again."[5]

Fox's early instinct that mysticism must lead not only to God but to a challenge of the injustice in society was obviously still strong, and it was clear that he saw the Roman Catholic Church as part of the structure that needed to be challenged. Valid prayer, in Fox's view, involves not only a response to God but involvement in social transformation. Those with such a viewpoint have never found it easy to maintain a comfortable relationship with institutions. Fox has called himself a "spiritual pyromaniac"[6]—and most institutions leave a great deal of dead wood around where a pyromaniac can cause trouble.

For ten years, however, the relationship between Fox and the Dominican Order and the Roman Catholic Church was quiet, if uneasy. Happily building his Institute, pursuing his studies, writing, speaking, and publishing, Fox was making himself known as a prophetic and accessible voice, someone with new things to say, someone who had a feel for the popular culture and who was able to get attention outside the walls of the church.

In 1976 a second book picked up where the first one left off. With an equally outrageous title, *Whee! We, wee All the Way Home*, and subtitled *A Guide to Sensual, Prophetic Spirituality*, it set out to do for mysticism what his first book had done for prayer: make it accessible to those who imagined that it was something only for cloistered monks and wild-eyed hermits. "This is a book," he wrote in the preface, "about waking up and returning to a biblical, justice-oriented spirituality." The front cover of the paperback edition shows young men and women huddled together and throwing their arms in the air in what might be interpreted either as an orgiastic dance or a victory celebration after a football game, while the back cover refers to Fox as "a crusader and a smasher of chains." Chapter headings include phrases like "how God is like an elephant," "large and unfriendly dragons," and "sensual spirituality." Scholarly quotations from Thomas Aquinas rub shoulders with citations from C. J. Jung, James Baldwin, Freud, Marx, and Einstein. The appeal to a mass audience was strong.

Conservatives in the church were unhappy with his references to drugs and eastern religions as avenues through which people seek mystical experience, nor could they take much comfort from the fact that Fox spoke positively of the now discarded Latin mass, since that too implies a challenge of authority. Mysticism, Fox argues, arises naturally out of the human experience of the created order. Institutionalized religion tends to substitute what Fox calls "tactical ecstasies"—strategies of experiencing God, such as chanting, fasting, and incense—for the direct experience of God in God's creation and so is apt to cut the mystical off from its roots. Ecstasy, the experience of standing outside oneself and in a deeper relationship with God, can become once again a familiar experience if we can learn anew to respond to nature and the sensual side of our being:

> [Ecstasy] happens not once a year or once a month but many times a day for a person who is awake and aware. That is, for the person who has learned to let go. For that person, God is everywhere and all is in God....Ecstasy is a breakthrough in our consciousness—an awareness of the unity of all things in God.[7]

In that last phrase, we become aware of a new factor in Fox's thought. "Breakthrough" was a term used in the fourteenth century by Meister Eckhart, a mystic whose life was strikingly parallel to the life of Matthew Fox. Eckhart too was a Dominican who had deliberately aimed his message at ordinary Christians; he too had spoken of "the unity of all things" and the awareness of God in all creation; and Eckhart had also been on a collision course with the Vatican. Now at last Fox had found Meister

Eckhart, his great predecessor, and a way of seeing that was deeply congenial. Fox shared Eckhart's sense that "if one really has God with one, one has God in all places, in the street and in the presence of everyone, just as well as in church, or the desert, or the cell,"[8] and, like Eckhart, had a way of putting things plainly in ways that appealed to ordinary Christians more than those in authority.

Though Eckhart was one of the best known of all Dominicans, oddly enough it was not until seventeen years after Fox first joined the Dominicans that he discovered Eckhart. Fox says he had been a Dominican for ten years before even hearing the name and that initially he "resisted reading Eckhart because numerous commentators on Eckhart had told me that he was basically a Neoplatonic mystic." That, Fox knew, was an approach that led to dualism, to divisions of all kinds—"of soul vs. body, of male vs. female, of intellect vs. creativity, of mysticism vs. politics." And this sort of dualism, he was "absolutely convinced...was the last thing the West needed."[9] Yet by different paths, Fox and Eckhart had come to the same way of thinking, and would experience similar conflicts with Roman authority as well.

At this point we probably need to stop and do a bit of theology. Why is it that both Fox and Eckhart in their attempt to communicate a deeper knowledge of God should run afoul of church authorities? We have said already that mystics and administrators are given different gifts. It is said that a third or more of all Americans have had some sort of "spiritual experience," but for most people such experience is rare; it may be a significant or even transforming moment but it remains outside the usual flow of their lives. For mystics, such experience is at the center of their lives but, as they try to tell others what they have known, words fail. God is beyond all our words; any attempt to use words is to limit God to the boundaries of our minds and our means of expression. And yet the mystic insists on trying; something so amazing, so overwhelming, must be talked about. And as the mystic tries to explain to others the experience he or she has had, the danger of exaggerating or oversimplifying becomes acute. "Mysticism," it has been said, "begins in mist and ends in schism." What begins in an experience beyond words ends with words the institutional church is unable to accept. The mystic's extravagant use of language challenges the carefully constructed systems of the rational theologian and the church, in a panic, disowns the mystic.

The special danger of mysticism (as the systematic theologians see it) is pantheism, the notion that everything is God. For mystics the experience of God is so total, finding God everywhere in all things, that they begin to suggest that there is no difference between God and all things. Angela of Foligno's description of her experience of God is characteristic:

> The eyes of my soul were opened, and I beheld the plenitude of God, wherein I did comprehend the whole world, both here and beyond the sea, and the abyss and ocean and all things. In all these things I beheld naught save the divine power, in a manner assuredly indescribable; so that through excess of marvelling the soul cried with a loud voice, saying, *This whole world is full of God.*[10]

Notice that word "indescribable," and the exuberant effort to describe it all the same. There lies the problem. Sober theologians would never deny that God the Creator is indeed present in all creation, but they insist that the Creator is not simply identified with creation. No, the Creator must transcend the creation; God is not only *in* all things but also *beyond* all things. Where the mystic tends to overemphasize the immanence of God, the systematic theologian may prefer to stress God's transcendence. As we noted earlier, the systematic theologian may also have some professional interests to protect: if God is in all things, perhaps the institutional church is not so important and the sacramental system is not so necessary. Church officials obviously will react badly to such ideas. And therein lies the root of the conflict between Eckhart, Fox, and the mystical tradition on the one hand, and the institutional church on the other.

Mysticism also recognizes a common bond with the same instinct in other religions since it speaks of a direct experience of God in all things. The Judeo-Christian tradition, however, centers our minds on the Bible, with its account of the history of a particular people and the unique events through which they came to understand God's will. Christianity holds up a particular revelation of God in the human person of Jesus Christ. When the Gospel according to St. John says "The true light, which enlightens everyone, was coming into the world" (1:9), it is attempting to reconcile these two very different points of view. On the one hand is "the true light" to be found in a particular person and tradition but, on the other hand, that same light "enlightens everyone"—all religions and philosophies have some knowledge of God. Here too the institutional church, designed to impart one official understanding of God's will, is often at cross-purposes with mysticism, with its experience of a truth that shines out from many lanterns.

Some mystics are desperate to share that experience with others. They clamor for attention. God is so real to them that they cannot imagine how people can go about business as usual. If only people could be made to see what they see, the world would be transformed. And if it requires exaggeration and oversimplification—orange bears with filmy wings floating over a field of flowers—then they will do it in order to share their vision. This too, threatens the institutional church, which prefers careful statements read by authorized persons at properly organized services on Sunday morning.

Eckhart in his day wrote of the presence of God in all creation, declared that there were many ways to the knowledge of God, and preached to ordinary peasants in the Rhone valley. When critics charged that his way of putting things might easily lead his listeners into error, he responded, "If the ignorant are not taught, they will never learn....The ignorant are taught in the hope of changing them from ignorant to enlightened people."[11] Likewise, Fox also began to say even more plainly that God was present in nature and sensual experience and the great religious traditions of the world: "Mysticism is, like art, a common language, uttering a common experience. There is only one great underground river, though there are numerous wells into it."[12] The seeds of future conflict were beginning to grow rapidly.

Meanwhile, Fox's reputation was spreading and he had decided to move his Institute to California. The computer industry had attracted many of the nation's leading scientists to the San

Francisco Bay area, and there he would have the opportunity for interaction with some of the most inquisitive minds of the burgeoning computer age. In 1983, the Institute was relocated to the grounds of Holy Names College in Oakland, a college directed by the Sisters of the Name Jesus and Mary. For his faculty Fox brought together a Zen master, a Yoruba priestess, a Jewish Sufi, a Lakota medicine man, a Nigerian drummer, and a self-professed witch named Starhawk. If there was but "one great underground river," students could let their buckets down in all these different wells and draw up the same fundamental truth.

But this blending of religious traditions was beginning to be too much for some of Matthew Fox's fellow Roman Catholics. Fox's next book, *Original Blessing*, fueled the controversy further. In contrast to the traditional Christian emphasis on original sin (which he did not deny), Fox pointed out that the Bible speaks of God's creation as originally good and suggested that the church had said too much about sin and not enough about creation's goodness.

Protesters and even picketers began to gather now when Fox came to speak. In Seattle a group called CUFF (Catholics United For the Faith) had demanded and obtained a Vatican investigation of Archbishop Hunthausen in Washington state. Fox also, they insisted, should be investigated and disciplined. When they came to his meetings to protest, Fox tried to reason with them but they spat on him. He began to get death threats in the mail. "Cosmic masses" at his Institute in Oakland were interrupted by angry protesters. Already the Vatican had assigned someone else to administer Archbishop Hunthausen's diocese and acted to silence theologians like Hans Küng in Germany, Charles Curran in Washington, and Leonardo Boff in Brazil.

Now that Fox had the Vatican's attention, they put pressure on his religious order to silence him as well. Cardinal Ratzinger, in charge of the Vatican Congregation of the Doctrine of the Faith, asked the Dominicans to conduct an investigation of Fox's activities and theology and report back. In an attempt to protect Fox and avoid a conflict, a committee of three Dominican theologians reported to Cardinal Ratzinger that they had found no heresy in

Fox's teaching but, rather, commended him for "his hard work and creativity." Ratzinger was not pleased; he found the conclusions of the committee "questionable" and said that there remained the basic question of "whether Father Fox should be permitted to publish at all."[13]

By the spring of 1988, after further exchanges, the Cardinal was in no mood for further delay. *Original Blessing*, he charged, was "dangerous and deviant. It is not in touch with authentic Christian spirituality and so it is far from the doctrine of the Magisterium."[14] An expert in canon law warned Fox that "taking on the Vatican is like standing in front of a train. You cannot win; no one ever has." Fox stepped down as director of the Institute and agreed to submit manuscripts of his books for review before publication. But the Cardinal demanded that further action be taken and the Master General wrote to Fox asking him to cease lecturing and preaching for a period of time.

Fox yielded, but not quietly. A public response to Ratzinger entitled "Is the Catholic Church Today a Dysfunctional Family?" was published in the Institute's journal and distributed to the press. The behavior of the Vatican, Fox wrote, was similar to that of a dysfunctional family whose members, attempting to appease an alcoholic father, become "'co-dependents.' Their silence sucks them into that very sickness that has so overtaken their violent father. Yet silence and denial prolong and intensify the suffering of everyone in the family." No one, Fox suggested, was telling Cardinal Ratzinger or the pope the truth they needed to hear: "For years I have been protecting you from the consequences of your behavior by remaining silent. To continue to do so would be sinful, for your behavior is becoming increasingly scandalous with greater and greater repercussions for the future of our church." He spoke of the church's "obsession with sex," "illusions of grandiosity," inability "to learn from past mistakes," "judgmentalism," "scapegoating," "refusal to engage in self-evaluation and self-criticism," and "signs of creeping fascism." "I pray," he concluded humbly, "that this letter might move you to listen and not just to condemn." Then, after a press conference in which he spoke of plans to travel and meet with another silenced theologian "perhaps at a party at which no one speaks," and having said enough to last him at least a year, he promised to remain silent for the next twelve months.

Surprisingly, four more years went by before Rome took definitive action. Fox returned from his year of silence and began his first public appearance with the words, "As I was saying...." " Nothing had really changed. If anything, a year of travel had widened Fox's horizons. He had spent time in silent retreat in Canada, made a Native American-style vision quest in the Cascade Mountains near Seattle, spent time with the previously silenced Leonardo Boff in Brazil (they did in fact speak to each other) and with the Sandanistas in Nicaragua. He had traveled also to Holland, France, Italy, and Greece. He had talked with theologians and he had visited the shrines of Marian devotion from the Middle Ages and of the goddess culture of ancient Greece. Refreshed and renewed by the experience, he was ready to suggest "a variety of reforms, including the granting of separate rites to Native Americans and African Americans, the creation of lay synods and the opening of full church ministry to women."[15] The United States, it seemed to him now, was lagging behind the rest of the Roman world in its willingness to press for change.

For the Dominican Order, however, change of a different sort was needed. Under constant pressure from Rome, they had to choose between defending Fox and preserving the order. Fox had already been told what would happen: he would be given an order he could not obey. Six months after his return, the Dominicans ordered him back to Chicago and in spite of appeals and delays and counter-appeals, he was dismissed from his order in March, 1993. In spite of the long struggle to stay in the church and the warnings Fox had been given of the inevitable outcome, the final decision came as a shock. What now? It seemed to Fox that he had three choices: to "hide under a rock," seek laicization, or move to another Christian tradition. To hide or give up his ministry was contrary to his deepest instincts; the one priest he consulted told him the Vatican was trying to isolate him and that he should find a way to stay within a larger community.

A year later, in April, 1994, Fox joined the Episcopal Church, characteristically following the service with a news conference.

The decision to come into the Anglican Communion was not easy. Fox had felt compelled to fight for ten years to keep his standing in the Church of Rome and he described his move as "bittersweet, not an easy decision at all."[16] Unlike parish priests, he had never lived daily with the consequences of *Humanae Vitae* and the ordinary work of a parish priest was something in which he had little interest. Of hearing confessions he said once, "I don't do windows." Fox's decision to change focused on particular issues of justice rather than on deeper issues of theology, as he stressed in his statement to the press on April 15, 1994:

> My decision to embrace the Anglican tradition is about in-cluding some anglo-saxon (and celtic) *common sense* into twenty-first century catholicism. I am speaking of course about *common sense* regarding married *and* unmarried clergy; about the common sense of ordaining women;...about the common sense of having a church structure that includes genuine participation of the laity as well as the clergy; of the common sense of endorsing birth control at a time when the human population explosion is threatening all life systems on this planet; of the common sense of openly discussing the contributions of lesbian and gay clergy; and the common sense of not granting to Rome itself so much power.[17]

"I believe," he added, "that the Episcopal Church, judging by the reception received so far to my request, is willing to take me and the vision I bring with me."

Missing from this statement is any attempt to spell out the fundamental relationship between the theology Fox had been developing and the characteristic position of Anglican theologi-ans with regard to Fox's central concerns: mysticism, social justice, Christian unity, and a creation-centered theology. There may be no such thing as Anglican theology, only Catholic theology, as John Mulryan's friend said to him, but there are characteristic Anglican emphases in theology that include most of the themes that have been important to Matthew Fox.

It seems likely that Fox was not very familiar with the broad nature of Anglicanism when he first applied for membership in the Episcopal Church. He says himself that "the single most important reason for my switch" was the openness of the Anglican Communion to experimental forms of liturgy, combined with an awareness of Anglican stands on "birth control, the ordination of women, lay participation, and decision making." In pursuing studies suggested by the diocese of California, Fox found in the work of theologians such as Richard Hooker, George Herbert, and Frederick Denison Maurice "ideas happily compatible with Creation Spirituality theology and my own Dominican tradition as developed in the persons of Thomas Aquinas and Meister Eckhart."[18] This "compatibility" extended to the broad themes of mysticism, social justice, Christian unity, and the central concern for creation.

Creation *and incarnation* have been central emphases in Anglican thought. Pere Chenu had taught Fox to balance a too-narrow fall/redemption theology with a creation-centered theology, but Chenu seems not to have balanced creation with incarnation, as Anglican theology typically has done. If the fall/redemption approach may be faulted for a tendency toward dualism, creation spirituality may equally be faulted for a tendency to ignore the particularity and concreteness of the biblical God revealed in historical events and in the life of Jesus of Nazareth.

The great Anglican theologians have insisted on this creation/ incarnation balance. Charles Gore, writing of the way God is revealed in creation, spoke of nature as "a progressive revelation of God culminating in Christ."[19] William Temple, carefully balancing immanence and transcendence, taught that "the whole process of that revelation which has been going on through nature, through history and through prophets, comes to complete fulfilment in the Incarnation."[20] It is that concreteness and particularity that tends to be missing in mysticism. Anglicanism cannot claim to be uniquely favorable to mysticism, but the same faith that produced the many great English mystics of pre-Reformation times—Julian of Norwich, Walter Hilton, Margery Kempe, Richard Rolle, and the unknown author of *The Cloud of Unknowing*—has produced in more recent times such extraordinary spiritual guides as Thomas Traherne, William Law, Nicholas Ferrar, and Evelyn Underhill.

Social justice is also a recurring theme in Anglicanism, perhaps because the Church of England, as an established church, has felt a responsibility to speak to the needs of the whole society. Bishop Latimer in the sixteenth century could stand before the king and call for justice for the poor; Jonathan Swift, dean of a cathedral in Dublin in the eighteenth century, could satirize his society's failures, while the nineteenth century brought the deep involvement of priests of the Oxford Movement in the lives of the poor in the bleak cities of the Industrial Revolution. In the twentieth century, names like Archbishop William Temple and Bishop Trevor Huddleston have been eclipsed only by the enormous publicity garnered by the Nobel prize-winning Archbishop Desmond Tutu of South Africa. In the United States, that tradition has continued to be a strong emphasis of the twentieth-century Episcopal Church, from the Christian socialists at the beginning of the century to controversial leaders like Presiding Bishop John Hines and New York Bishop Paul Moore in the sixties and seventies.

An emphasis on the doctrine of creation, which is so closely related to the mystic's awareness of God in all things, has, as Fox rightly points out, always been a central teaching of the great theologians. He cites Thomas Aquinas's "an error concerning the Creation ends as false thinking about God" and the Anglican poet-mystic Thomas Traherne's well-known passage from *Centuries*:

> You never enjoy the world aright till the sea itself floweth in your veins, till you are clothed with the heavens, and crowned with the stars; and perceive yourself to be the sole heir of the whole world, and more than so, because men are in it who are every one sole heirs as well as you.[21]

The mystical view that sees God *in* all things is always in danger of becoming pantheism, of identifying God *with* all things, and needs to be corrected, as Anglican theologians have tended to do, by an emphasis on the incarnation. But mystics are not always inclined to be careful and the church must choose whether to live with them and learn from them, balancing their overstatements with more careful theology, or to condemn them and lose the freshness and exuberance and insight they alone can bring to the church's constant need for renewal.

Anglicanism may be more tolerant of this kind of thinking than other traditions because of its emphasis on creation and incarnation. The medieval church stressed the sinfulness of human beings and preached about the danger of judgment, while the struggles of the Reformation seemed to strengthen that emphasis both in the Reformed tradition and in the Roman Catholic Church. Perhaps the English Channel gave the Church of England a sufficient sense of security in its separation from continental divisions to enable it to take a more optimistic view of the world and to think first of the goodness of creation and of God's love for us in entering it.

One Episcopal theologian, the late Terry Holmes, claimed that "this is the beginning point of Christian belief for the Anglican: the doctrine of creation....The material world is good....To know creation is to know God for those who can look beyond the landscape to the inner reality." Speaking of the dangers that theologians see in mysticism, he added:

> There is a real risk that this contemplation of creation, which is consistent with Christianity if understood rightly, can become pantheism....The protection against pantheism lies in the ability to see the purpose of God working in and through creation, and yet incomplete in and not infrequently thwarted by nature.[22]

Fox himself is careful to use a word modern Anglican theologians are also fond of: *panentheism*, God is in all things but not identical with all things. Nonetheless, enthusiasm for the revelation of God in nature can be overdone. To suggest, as Fox does, that every seminary, church, and synagogue should have a sweat lodge on its property and that a liturgical year might be dedicated to the mysteries of the human body with a "Liver Sunday...Spleen Sunday...Brain Sunday...Pancreas Sunday,"[23] and so on is probably unrealistic. It may not be good liturgy—or good theology either. But heretical? Not hardly.

No theologian this side of hereafter can be expected to provide us with a perfectly balanced statement of God's nature and our redemption. Aquinas was probably too rational, Augustine too sin-centered, Temple too philosophical, and so on. It is in the harmonies—and occasional dissonances—of a variety of voices that the truth is to be glimpsed, not in a carefully regulated monotone. Anglicanism has often been described as a faith that seeks, in the midst of competing voices, to find a middle way, a *via media*, between extremes. That might seem to have no appeal for Matthew Fox, who has written of God as "an extremist" and has called for "a spirituality of extremes,"[24] but Charles Simeon, a nineteenth century Anglican scholar, noted that "truth often lies not in the mean point between two extremes, but at both extremes!"

We should also be careful not to dismiss Fox, as some have done, as a "New Age guru." Fox is very clear about the difference between the faith he teaches and New Age spiritualism. There is, he has written, "distortion...in certain trends in the New Age movement which are...all consciousness and no conscience; all mysticism and no prophecy; all past life experiences, angelic encounters, untold bliss, and no critique of injustice or acknow-ledgment of the suffering and death that the toll of time takes. In short, no body. To these movements the Cosmic Christ says, 'Easter time. Behold my wounds. Love your neighbor. Set the captives free.'"[25] It is the wounds of the incarnate Jesus that must always balance the universality of the cosmic Christ.

Perhaps more important than exact theological agreement is a religious tradition unafraid of mystics, prophets, and even heretics, a tradition more afraid of authoritarianism than of freedom. "Legitimate authority," a recent essay on authority in the Anglican communion tells us, "is the direct opposite of coercive power."[26] Legitimate authority should nurture and cultivate. Such an approach cannot always provide quick and precise answers to every question; it is more concerned to leave room for growth and to adapt to the needs of a changing world. So the Episcopal Church is often torn by debate and seems indecisive and unable to speak clearly, but such tolerance of diversity is in the long run a strength. "Clarity of authority," warned one Anglican theologian, "should not be expected—in fact, it should be suspect—when we are attempting to make clear the infinite mind of God for the finite minds of humankind. When Anglicanism is true to its concept of authority, this apparent hesitance to say, *Thus saith the Lord!*...is not a sign of weakness, but evidence of strength and wisdom."[27]

It is a church with such confident strength that has found a place for Matthew Fox and so many other explorers who seek a deeper knowledge of God and who ought to be welcomed and encouraged in that search.

Notes

The general outline of Matthew Fox's life is drawn from the following sources: Lawrence Stone, "More Joy! The Passionate Priesthood of Father Matthew Fox," in *Utne Reader* (March/April 1992); Lawrence Stone, "Matthew Fox Rolls Away the Stone," in *Saints and Sinners* (New York: Alfred A. Knopf, 1993); and Matthew Fox, *Confessions: The Making of a Post-Denominational Priest* (San Francisco: HarperSanFrancisco, 1996).

1. Matthew Fox, *Confessions: The Making of a Post-Denominational Priest* (San Francisco: HarperSanFrancisco, 1996), p. 52.

2. *Ibid.*, pp. 69–70.

3. Matthew Fox, *On Becoming a Musical, Mystical Bear* (New York: Paulist Press, 1972), p. xxix.

4. *Ibid.*, p. 50.

5. *Ibid.*, pp. xxviii, 22.

6. Fox, *Confessions*, p. 151.

7. Matthew Fox, *Whee! We, wee All the Way Home* (Santa Fe: Bear & Co., 1981), p. 17.

8. Matthew Fox, *Breakthrough: Meister Eckhart's Creation Spirituality in New Translation*, with Introduction and Commentaries by Matthew Fox (Garden City, N.Y.: Image Books, 1980), p. 6.

9. *Ibid.*

10. Evelyn Underhill, *Mysticism* (New York: The Noonday Press, 1955), p. 252. (The Latin really says "pregnant with God.")

11. Raymond Bernard Blakney, *Meister Eckhart: A Modern Translation* (New York: Harper & Brothers, 1941), p. xxiii.

12. Matthew Fox, *The Coming of the Cosmic Christ* (HarperSanFrancisco, 1988), p. 230.

13. Unless otherwise noted, quotations and chronology for this period of Fox's life are drawn from "Is the Catholic Church Today a Dysfunctional Family?: A Pastoral Letter to Cardinal Ratzinger and the Whole Church from Matthew Fox, O.P.," published in *Creation* (November/December, 1988), pp. 23-37.

14. Fox, *Confessions*, p. 168.

15. "Unrepentant Fox Seeks People's Church," *National Catholic Reporter* (February 16, 1990).

16. "Fox Move to Episcopal Church 'Bittersweet,'" *National Catholic Reporter* (April 29, 1994).

17. Statement from Matthew Fox, April 15, 1994.

18. Quoted from a personal letter of July 13, 1995.

19. Charles Gore, *The Incarnation of the Son of God* (New York: Charles Scribner's Sons, 1891), p. xii.

20. William Temple, *Mens Creatrix* (London: MacMillan, 1923), p. 317.

21. Fox, *Whee! We, wee*, pp. 37, 45-46.

22. Urban T. Holmes III, *What is Anglicanism?* (Wilton, Conn.: Morehouse-Barlow, 1982), pp. 27-28.

23. Fox, *Coming of the Cosmic Christ*, pp. 239, 222-223.

24. Fox, *Whee! We, wee*, pp. 110-111.

25. Fox, *Coming of the Cosmic Christ*, p. 141.

26. John Skinner, "Ideology, Authority, and Faith," in Stephen Sykes, ed., *Authority in the Anglican Communion* (Toronto: Anglican Book Centre, 1987), p. 33.

27. Holmes, *What is Anglicanism?*, p. 16.

7

In Search of the Catholic Church

The Anglican Communion is a fellowship of Churches at one and the same time Catholic in seeking to do justice to the wholeness of Christian truth, in emphasizing continuity through the Episcopate, and in retaining the historic Creeds and Sacraments of undivided Christendom; and Evangelical in its commission to proclaim the Gospel and in its emphasis on personal faith in Jesus Christ as Savior.

(The Anglican Congress, 1954)

"The Episcopal Church is a Catholic Church in love with freedom." *(the Rt. Rev. Paul Moore)*

The stories told in this book were not scientifically selected, but are simply stories of people I happened to know or to be told of by others. So there has been no attempt to obtain a statistically balanced sample of former Roman Catholics in the Episcopal Church today, and these stories may or may not be typical. But the life of the church is a story, not statistics, and it is from stories primarily that we learn. No other stories will be exactly like these and it may be—though it seems unlikely—that no other stories have anything in common with these.

But these are true stories; they are part of the larger story of the Episcopal Church, indeed of the Christian church, and by paying attention to them we may be able to learn something useful about how new members come to the church and become part of the church, about evangelism and incorporation. We may also learn something about the Episcopal Church, since newcomers often have a clearer view of the church's reality than those who are so used to its familiar outlines that they no longer really see them. And we may learn something about what is happening today—in other words, what God is doing in our history, both secular and sacred.

First, evangelism.

They used to tell stories in Japan of an American missionary who spent all his time standing in one of the major train stations in Tokyo preaching in English to the thousands of bemused Japanese passing by. His theory was that God would interpret for him and would enable those who were chosen to hear the Word and respond in spite of the language barrier.

The picture many people have of evangelism is not very different from that. We think of evangelism all too often as preaching on street corners and buttonholing unsuspecting passers-by. And for most of us, that is probably not an appealing picture. We have no desire to do it and are most unlikely to respond to those who do. Indeed, most of us have probably come upon an evangelist preaching somewhere on a street corner and paid about as much attention as we would if the evangelist were speaking Japanese.

Nevertheless, Episcopalians are deeply conflicted about evangelism. We see churches around us engaging in evangelism and appearing to grow. We have a certain respect for Billy Graham and may even have become involved in one of his crusades at one time in our lives. Furthermore, we love our church and we want it to prosper. And so we feel we ought to be actively engaged in evangelism, going out and pushing our faith at others, however distasteful the exercise may be to us and to them.

But in the stories I have told there is not a trace of that kind of evangelism. Only Kelly Merlo was specifically invited to join anything, and that was a neighborhood Bible study which took place in an Episcopal Church. But even so, she was never specifically invited to attend that church and did so finally out of a desire to learn more about the church that sponsored the group she had joined.

So how did these people find the Episcopal Church? Four of them, it might be said, "married into the family." But when they did, that family was reticent in the extreme. Dan Adams and Jim Gordon were both Episcopalians, but when each of them married a Roman Catholic they stopped going to the Episcopal Church and eventually became Roman Catholics. When Hope Adams and Teresa Gordon finally lost all patience with the Roman Catholic Church, it was logical for them to move to a church they already knew in part because of their spouse's upbringing in that church. Jane Onstad kept going to the Episcopal Church, but neither she nor her father, an Episcopal priest, pushed their faith at Jerry Lamb: Jerry turned naturally to his wife's church when he realized how much he needed a Christian community, because he had learned very casually and without any pressure what the Episcopal Church stood for. It wouldn't have worked if they had pressed him, and they seemed to know it. Steve Roman and his fiancee checked out several Roman Catholic churches first with the assumption that they would find a Roman Catholic church that satisfied them both. But when Steve began attending Chris's church he found the kind of freedom and stimulus to grow that he had found in Roman Catholic chaplaincy programs in school and college but could not find in a local Roman church.

Three more of the stories tell of a rather similar kind of evangelism. Jerry Gallagher and Colleen McMahon Sica turned to the Episcopal Church because they already had some sense of what it stood for. They had picked up that knowledge in the course of theological studies, casual conversations with Episco-palians, and general reading. John Mulryan also had heard of the Episcopal Church, but he quite literally stumbled into it because it was there. All three came because of a specific crisis in their lives: John Mulryan's wife was critically ill; Jerry Gallagher needed a place to get married; and Colleen McMahon Sica needed a place to bring her children for religious education. The Roman Catholic Church was no longer a live option for them and they had a vague sense that the Episcopal Church could meet their needs.

A similar story, and probably more common, is that of Janet Gagnon, who came to the Episcopal Church looking for a church in which to get married. Having been divorced, she no longer felt welcome in the Roman Catholic Church and her sister suggested that she would be comfortable with the Episcopal Church because the worship seemed so similar.

Two stories tell of individuals who came to the Episcopal Church because they became involved in programs of the church and then decided to see what else the church that sponsored those programs had to offer. Kelly Merlo was invited to join a Bible study group by a friend and Patti O'Kane was told that Integrity might offer more than Dignity. Neither of them was specifically looking for a church—though they had some problems with the Roman Catholic Church—but they found a program they valued and then discovered behind the program a church that offered them more opportunity to grow.

The story of Matthew Fox may be most similar to the stories of those who needed a church in a crisis and for whom the Roman Catholic Church was no longer a live option. Having been silenced by his own church and then expelled by his Dominican Order, it was not surprising that he would begin to look around. Being a theologian, it was natural that he had already encountered Anglican theologians and Anglican spirituality and that he knew something at least of how nearly their thinking corresponded with his.

There are several different patterns here, but in every case the initiative was with the individual looking for a church, not with the church and its members. In a deeper sense, of course, the initiative was with the Holy Spirit who had been at work in these lives for many years. The role of the Episcopal Church was to be sensitive to the work of the Spirit and to support that work by being sensitive to the individual, supporting each of them in their pilgrimage without either pushing or pulling.

Am I suggesting that the Episcopal Church does not or should not engage in evangelism? Far from it. What seems evident from these stories is that our common picture of evangelism is far too narrow. Martin Smith, SSJE, likes to say that we have allowed certain churches to define the word "conversion" for us and have lost sight of the range of experience which it includes. So, too, with the closely related word "evangelism": we have allowed these churches to persuade us that if we are not engaged in their narrow kind of evangelism, we are not engaged in evangelism at all.

The pattern of aggressive evangelism which these churches practice is rather like fishing. You bait a hook and drop it in the water, or tie a fly to your line and cast it out, and you hope that a hungry fish will pass by. If it happens to do so, and you tighten the line at exactly the right moment, you can, in a brief and violent action, haul the fish to the boat or bank. The nets that Jesus' disciples used are not very different in this respect: fishing nets thrown into the sea may or may not happen to enclose a school of fish. There is more than one way to catch fish, but there is in all of them a large element of chance, and a degree of violence in taking the fish out of its natural element against its will. If the analogy can be pushed this far, these stories have to do with a kind of evangelism that allows individuals to remain "in the water" while providing nourishment and enabling them to grow in a natural and appropriate way, without doing violence to their lives.

The evangelism, the "fishing," done by the Episcopal Church in these stories is then primarily a matter of being there, of simply being the kind of church these individuals could come to for nourishment when they failed to find it where they were. The trauma of change is located in the decision to leave the Roman Church far more than in coming into the Episcopal Church. But that is in the nature of these two kinds of Catholicism. Rome has traditionally presented itself to its members as the only true church, while Anglicanism has claimed only to be one expression of the Catholic tradition. It is traumatic to leave the "only" true church; it need not be traumatic to come into a church which feels comfortable and makes no claim of a monopoly on the truth.

First of all, then, we need to begin with a broad definition of conversion. If we think of conversion as a continuing process of spiritual growth, most of these stories do not have to do with the first step in the conversion process, from non-faith to faith. Since we set out to tell the stories of Roman Catholics who became Episcopalians, we have ruled out stories of that sort of conversion anyway. Rather, as has been the case, we should expect to hear of people who were believing Christians who felt that their growth in faith was being blocked where they were and who found a place in which they could continue to grow. Their "conversion" from one church to another, then, is simply one more step in a process but one which opens up new possibilities of growth in a continuing Christian life.

One story, in this perspective, may stand out as different. The visitors who came to Tony Merlo's doorstep were concerned with a more fundamental and primary kind of conversion, a saving personal relationship with Jesus Christ. That kind of focus, usually found in Episcopal churches which make active evangelism their primary mission, can be very effective but it may not give enough recognition to the fact that God has already long been at work in the lives of those they evangelize. Tony Merlo could not affirm a personal relationship with Jesus Christ, but he had been reading his Bible more faithfully than most churchgoers and was already, in many ways, a believing and practicing Christian. Even here, however, the Merlos were able to respond readily to the Episcopal Church not because it was radically different from the church they had known, but because it was not. Even here, overt evangelism relied on the church being there and being recognizably the Catholic church.

Another convert, one who came into the Episcopal Church from "the other side," the evangelical tradition, put it this way:

> The church...sits like a great stone cathedral heavy on the earth—the great, unarguing church. She does not insist on her own importance, and like her Lord, she does not answer back. Simply by being what she is, she summons all who will to step through her always open doors. What is this strange attraction, this mysterious magnetism? It is only that she exalts her Lord, raising up before us all the one who said, "And I, when I am lifted up from the earth will draw all men to myself" (John 12:32).[1]

This "strange attraction" may also help to explain why there is rather little explicit theology in the stories we have told. In the first place, none of the individuals whose stories have been told was moving from non-faith to faith. Conversion, in that primary or preliminary sense, as we have said, was not the issue. What was at issue was the way the faith was presented, and therefore the emphasis may seem to fall on external matters like the quality of the music or the warmth of the welcome. But these are the soil in which faith grows. A garden book will usually spend more time talking about compost and cultivating than the plants because, given the right conditions, the plants will take care of themselves. Perhaps faith, too, is like that. It is expressed in many different ways, and the church's role is often not so much to lecture on theology as to provide compost and cultivation, the soil in which faith can develop its fullest growth.

Rowan Williams, the Bishop of Monmouth in Wales, speaks of the *"oblique* character of the Christian knowledge of God":

> We do not begin from innate or intuitive ideas of the absolute or the transcendent; we are drawn into a transformed life, speech, and activity in which the inexhaustible resource of the God who draws us is gradually discovered.[2]

We do not begin with theology, and no theologian—not even Augustine or Thomas Aquinas or Meister Eckhart or Karl Barth—will provide a way of thinking useful to everyone. Rather, we are drawn into a community in which the "depth of the riches and wisdom and knowledge of God" (Rom. 11:33) is gradually discovered in experiences which remain always beyond our ability to articulate and express.

Second, about "Catholicism." The word "catholic" means "universal." St. Vincent of Lerins, in the fifth century, defined it as being "that which has been believed everywhere, always and by all." Does such a Catholicism exist? Certainly there are very few things—if any—that have been believed everywhere, always, and by everyone. In the seventeenth century an English priest, attempting to describe the Catholic church, wrote an account of a man shipwrecked on a remote island called Soteria off the coast of China. In that imaginary island he had found a church "not to be paralleled...in the known world if a steady adherence to the apostolical doctrine and discipline in their original purity, and a strict conformity of practice and profession, may be allowed to be the glory of a Church."[3]

Perhaps that illustrates the point: a strict insistence on St. Vincent's definition points us to a Catholicism which, though we long for it and often claim to possess it, cannot be found in the real world. George Tavard, a Roman Catholic scholar who made a study of Anglicanism, suggests that Catholicism as some of the greatest Anglicans have defined it is "less a fact than a hope." He quotes William Nicolls, who wrote that Catholicism is

> a dynamic quality, not a static possession. It is a continual pressing forward to the historical realization of that in which we participate eschatologically, that Body of Christ in which the Spirit makes us members now, into whose fullness we shall have grown up only in the Kingdom.[4]

It is, as we have seen, characteristic of Anglicanism to avoid easy definitions. Catholicism can be defined to some extent by the life of the church in the past, but the church continues to grow and develop. In the long view of history, the two millennia of church history may be the whole story or only a brief beginning; it may well be, as others have suggested, that we are still in the early days of the church and therefore cannot see clearly what it is God has been doing in our midst. In this young and growing church, still unsure of itself and its mission, we look to our traditions for security. Roman Catholics hold fast to the unity provided by the papacy. Anglicans prefer the unity to be found in the episcopate, the *Book of Common Prayer*, and the fundamentals held by almost all Christians almost everywhere most of the time: the Bible, the Nicene Creed, and the two central sacraments of baptism and the eucharist. Protestants generally are content with an inward unity while differing greatly in organization, worship, and doctrine. Nevertheless, the twentieth century has been, on balance, a time of hope for a deeper Christian unity. Certainly there has been more cooperation and dialogue than in many centuries. And although the tensions within the churches seem frequently to be on the verge of producing new schisms, there have been some notable steps toward fuller unity.

In particular, the Roman and Anglican churches have been involved in an ongoing search for the meaning of the Catholic tradition in our own day. Both in the United States and on an international level, Anglican and Roman Catholic theologians have been meeting to seek agreement on basic doctrines and to search for a way toward greater unity. These discussions have led to several agreed statements. And while national and international discussions proceed, there has been progress as well at a local level where some Roman Catholic and Episcopal parishes have entered into covenant agreements to work together and pray for each other.

Simultaneously, however, developments within each church seem to be producing new divisions, both within them and between them. The Vatican, for example, has been putting new emphasis on the idea of papal infallibility, which is perhaps the most divisive issue of all. Although the exact meaning of the doctrine of papal infallibility has never been clearly spelled out, it inevitably casts a shadow over all papal statements and, indeed, all teaching within the Roman Catholic Church. The scope for questioning and probing is reduced within that church and the reluctance of non-Roman Catholics to move closer to a church so constricted is inevitably increased. The difficulty involved was highlighted late in 1995 when the Congregation for the Doctrine of the Faith asserted that papal teaching on the inadmissibility of ordaining women was infallible. Since the pope himself had not said his teaching on the subject was infallible, it raised the question whether, when an organ of the Vatican says a papal statement is infallible, it says it infallibly.

Also of concern is the growing Roman Catholic practice of allowing lay people ("lay eucharistic ministers") to administer communion in the absence of a priest. Lay eucharistic ministers in the Episcopal Church always function within the context of the eucharistic liturgy: they assist a priest in administering communion and take the sacrament directly from the altar to the sick. They do not conduct services at which the sacrament is distributed. However, the increasing shortage of priests in the Roman Catholic Church makes it difficult in some areas to provide a priest to say mass, so the custom has emerged of a priest visiting a church and consecrating enough bread and wine to last until he can come again, and a lay person regularly conducting a service of the Word and distributing the consecrated elements.

To many, such a practice twists the ancient pattern of Christian worship beyond recognition. The eucharist is a corporate action in which Christians come together to participate in Christ's death and resurrection and, in so doing, to share Christ's own life in the bread and wine. The eucharist is an action in which Christians become who they are: the body of Christ. A service of the Word in which the elements are distributed is something fundamentally different. It makes of the service a handing out of packaged grace to passive recipients rather than a community event in and through which all are nourished.

This pattern may be easier for Roman Catholics to accept because until relatively recently the mass was said in Latin while worshipers said their own private devotions. Vatican II attempted to correct the balance by translating the mass into the language of the people and moving altars out from the wall so that the corporate nature of the action could be recognized. But the old misunderstandings are still very much present, reinforced now in those places where a shortage of priests makes corporate action difficult.

In the same way that a shortage of priests has begun to distort the basic pattern of the eucharist, so the denial of ordination to women has begun to distort the pattern of ministry. One hears of "community masses" and "house churches" and even of convents where the mass is celebrated by lay people for lack of a priesthood shared between men and women. If the priesthood is not open to all, some have opted to do without it or make their own and so in the name of "Catholic tradition" new divisions are created. The word "Catholic" becomes identified with what seems more like narrowness than universality.

So we come to the end of the twentieth century with two great churches defining themselves as "Catholic" yet unable to agree on the meaning and implications of that word. Anyone entering a church or attending a service in either tradition can easily see that a common heritage has shaped them but the Roman Church's insistence on papal authority and its positions on social-sexual issues like abortion and birth control and divorce and the ordination of women keeps Anglicans (and others) at a distance, while the papacy insists that the positions other churches have taken on these same issues make ecumenical progress increasingly difficult for the Church of Rome.

Inevitably, then, individuals must find their own way into the form of Catholicism that seems most likely to enable them to grow in grace—as those whose stories we have told have done. But the necessity for these journeys creates mixed feelings for at least some Episcopalians. Roger White, for example, writes in a letter that "while I am THRILLED that [Steve Roman] is at St. Andrew's, I confess to sadness that so strong a Christian needed to 'leave home.'" And Dean Alan Jones, who sponsored Matthew Fox's entrance into the Episcopal Church, spoke of a sense of excitement about Fox's "ability to reach people in new ways," but also of a sense that "when someone can't be at home in another tradition, we all lose."[5] That sense of loss must continue to fuel the search for a fuller understanding of God's will for the Catholic church universal, and a deeper unity in that vision.

Notes

1. Robert Webber, *Evangelicals on the Canterbury Trail* (Waco, Tx.: Word Books, 1985), p. 100.

2. Rowan Williams, *The Wound of Knowledge* (Cambridge, Mass.: Cowley Publications, 1990), p. 52.

3. George H. Tavard, *The Quest for Catholicity* (London: Burns and Oates, 1963), p. 121.

4. *Ibid.*, p. 206.

5. *San Jose Mercury News* (April 15, 1994).

Cowley Publications is a ministry of the Society of St. John the Evangelist, a religious community for men in the Episcopal Church. Emerging from the Society's tradition of prayer, theological reflection, and diversity of mission, the press is centered in the rich heritage of the Anglican Communion.

Cowley Publications seeks to provide books, audio cassettes, and other resources for the ongoing theological exploration and spiritual development of the Episcopal Church and others in the body of Christ. To this end, it is dedicated to developing a new generation of theological writers, encouraging them to produce timely, creative, and stimulating publications of excellence, and making these publications available widely, reaching both clergy and lay persons.